Congressional Research Service

Social Security Reform: Current Issues and Legislation

Dawn Nuschler
Specialist in Income Security

November 28, 2012

Congressional Research Service

7-5700

www.crs.gov

RL33544

CRS Report for Congress ————————————————————
Prepared for Members and Committees of Congress

Summary

Social Security reform has been an area of interest to policymakers for many years. In 2011, Social Security program changes were discussed during negotiations on legislation to increase the federal debt limit and reduce federal budget deficits. In August 2011, the Budget Control Act of 2011 (P.L. 112-25) established a Joint Select Committee on Deficit Reduction tasked with recommending ways to reduce the deficit by at least $1.5 trillion over the fiscal year period 2012 to 2021. Social Security program changes were among the measures discussed by the Joint Committee. The Joint Committee, however, did not reach agreement on a legislative proposal by the November 23, 2011, statutory deadline. Currently, Social Security program changes may be considered as part of a deficit reduction package under negotiation by policymakers.

The spectrum of ideas for reform ranges from relatively minor changes to the pay-as-you-go social insurance system enacted in the 1930s to a redesigned, "modernized" program based on personal savings and investments modeled after IRAs and 401(k)s. Proponents of the fundamentally different approaches to reform cite varying policy objectives that go beyond simply restoring long-term financial stability to the Social Security system. They cite objectives that focus on improving the adequacy and equity of benefits, as well as those that reflect different philosophical views about the role of the Social Security program and the federal government in providing retirement income. However, the system's projected long-range financial outlook provides a backdrop for much of the Social Security reform debate in terms of the timing and degree of recommended program changes.

On April 23, 2012, the Social Security Board of Trustees released it latest projections showing that the trust funds will be exhausted in 2033 and that an estimated 75% of scheduled annual benefits will be payable with incoming receipts at that time (under the intermediate projections). The primary reason is demographics. Between 2010 and 2030, the number of people aged 65 and older is projected to increase by 77%, while the number of workers supporting the system is projected to increase by 7%. In addition, the trustees project that the system will run a cash flow deficit in each year of the 75-year projection period. When current Social Security tax revenues are insufficient to pay benefits and administrative costs, federal securities held by the trust funds are redeemed and Treasury makes up the difference with other receipts. When there are no surplus governmental receipts, policymakers have three options: raise taxes or other income, reduce other spending, or borrow from the public (or a combination of these options).

Public opinion polls show that less than 50% of respondents are confident that Social Security can meet its long-term commitments. There is also a public perception that Social Security may not be as good a value for future retirees. These concerns, and a belief that the nation must increase national savings, have led to proposals to redesign the system. At the same time, others suggest that the system's financial outlook is not a "crisis" in need of immediate action. Supporters of the current program structure point out that the trust funds are projected to have a positive balance until 2033 and that the program continues to have public support and could be affected adversely by the risk associated with some of the reform ideas. They contend that only modest changes are needed to restore long-range solvency to the Social Security system.

During the 111th Congress, four Social Security reform measures were introduced. None of the measures received congressional action. In the 112th Congress, several Social Security reform measures have been introduced; none have received congressional action.

Contents

Figures

Tables

Contacts

Background

Social Security reform is an issue of ongoing interest to policymakers. In 2011, Social Security program changes were discussed during negotiations on legislation to increase the federal debt limit and reduce federal budget deficits. The Budget Control Act of 2011 (P.L. 112-25), which was signed by President Obama on August 2, 2011, established a Joint Select Committee on Deficit Reduction. The Joint Committee was tasked with recommending ways to reduce the deficit by at least $1.5 trillion over the fiscal year period 2012 to 2021. Social Security program changes were among the measures considered by the Joint Committee, however, no agreement was reached on a legislative proposal by the November 23, 2011, statutory deadline. Currently, Social Security program changes may be considered as part of a deficit reduction package under negotiation by policymakers.

The Social Security reform debate reflects different approaches to reform. Some policymakers support restructuring the program through the creation of individual accounts (i.e., a pre-funded system in which benefits would be based increasingly on personal savings and investments). Supporters of individual accounts point to the system's projected long-range funding shortfall as a driver for change in conjunction with creating a system that would give workers a sense of "ownership" of their retirement savings. Other policymakers support maintaining the current structure of the program (i.e., a defined benefit system funded on a pay-as-you-go basis), pointing to the system's projected long-range financial outlook to support their view that the system is not in immediate "crisis" and that only modest program changes may be needed.

Proponents of the fundamentally different approaches to reform (ranging from relatively minor changes to the current pay-as-you-go social insurance system to the creation of a "modernized" program based on personal savings and investments modeled after IRAs and 401(k)s) cite varying policy objectives that go beyond simply restoring long-term financial stability to the system. They cite objectives that focus on improving the adequacy and equity of benefits, as well as those that reflect different philosophical views about the role of the Social Security program and the federal government in providing retirement income. However, the system's projected long-range financial outlook provides a backdrop for much of the Social Security reform debate in terms of the timing and degree of recommended program changes. For example, one of the key criteria used to evaluate any reform proposal is its projected impact on the Social Security trust funds. To place the discussion of Social Security reform issues into context, the report first looks at Social Security program financing and the long-range projections for the Social Security trust funds as reported by the Social Security Board of Trustees.[1] The report then looks at the various objectives and proposals for reform.

---

[1] The Social Security Board of Trustees is composed of three officers of the President's Cabinet (the Secretary of the Treasury, the Secretary of Labor, and the Secretary of Health and Human Services), the Commissioner of Social Security, and two public representatives who are appointed by the President and subject to confirmation by the Senate. The trustees report annually on the financial status of the trust funds based on three sets of assumptions (low cost, intermediate and high cost) given the uncertainty surrounding projections for a 75-year period. The projections discussed in this CRS report are the intermediate (or "best estimate") projections from the 2012 trustees report (see The 2012 Annual Report of the Board of Trustees of the Federal Old-Age and Survivors Insurance and Federal Disability Insurance Trust Funds, April 23, 2012, available at http://www.socialsecurity.gov/OACT/TR/2012/).

Social Security Program Financing

Social Security, one of the largest federal programs, is a social insurance system that pays benefits to retired or disabled workers, their family members, and to the family members of deceased workers. As of September 2012, there were 56.4 million Social Security beneficiaries. Approximately 65% of those beneficiaries were retired workers and 16% were disabled workers. The remaining beneficiaries were survivors, or the spouses and children of retired or disabled workers.[2] Currently, Social Security covers an estimated 159.7 million workers.[3]

The Social Security program is funded by payroll taxes paid by covered workers and their employers, federal income taxes paid by some beneficiaries on a portion of their benefits, and interest income from the Social Security trust fund investments. Social Security tax revenues are invested in interest-bearing federal government securities (special issues) held by the Old-Age, Survivors, and Disability Insurance (OASDI) trust funds maintained by the U.S. Treasury Department.[4] The revenues exchanged for the federal government securities are deposited into the Treasury's general fund and are indistinguishable from revenues in the general fund that come from other sources. Funds needed to pay Social Security benefits and administrative expenses come from the redemption or sale of federal government securities held by the trust funds.[5]

To place Social Security's finances into perspective, in 2011, the Social Security trust funds had receipts totaling $805 billion, expenditures totaling $736 billion, and a total surplus (a surplus including interest income) of $69 billion. The trust funds had a cash flow deficit (a deficit excluding interest income) of $45 billion. At the end of 2011, the Social Security trust funds held assets totaling $2.7 trillion.[6] Because the assets held by the trust funds are federal government securities, the trust fund balance ($2.7 trillion in 2011) represents the amount of money owed to the Social Security trust funds by the general fund of the U.S. Treasury.

Social Security Financing on a Cash Flow Basis

From 1984 to 2009, Social Security generated surplus tax revenues. Surplus tax revenues and interest income credited to the trust funds in the form of federal government securities contributed to a growing trust fund balance. **Table 1** shows the amount of annual surplus Social Security tax revenues collected by the federal government and used for other (non-Social Security) purposes from 1984 to 2009. Surplus Social Security tax revenues totaled $1.21 trillion (in nominal dollars) from 1984 to 2009. **Table 1** also shows total annual Social Security surpluses (including interest income) from 1984 to 2009.

---

[2] Social Security Administration (SSA), *Monthly Statistical Snapshot, September 2012*, Table 2. The latest edition of the *Monthly Statistical Snapshot* is at http://www.socialsecurity.gov/policy/docs/quickfacts/stat_snapshot/index.html.

[3] SSA, *2012 Social Security/SSI/Medicare Information*, April 25, 2012, p. 1, http://www.socialsecurity.gov/legislation/2012_FactSheet.pdf.

[4] OASDI is the formal name for Social Security. There are two separate trust funds: the Old-Age and Survivors Insurance (OASI) trust fund and the Disability Insurance (DI) trust fund. This report refers to the two trust funds on a combined basis as the Social Security trust funds.

[5] SSA, Trust Fund FAQs, http://www.ssa.gov/OACT/ProgData/fundFAQ.html.

[6] SSA, Trust Fund Data, http://www.ssa.gov/OACT/STATS/table4a3.html.

At the end of 2011, the trust funds were credited with assets totaling $2.7 trillion. Under the intermediate assumptions of the 2012 trustees report, the trust fund balance is projected to continue to increase, peaking at $3.1 trillion (in nominal dollars) at the end of 2020 ($2.5 trillion in constant 2012 dollars). Beginning in 2021, however, program expenditures are projected to exceed total income (tax revenues plus interest income) and trust fund assets will begin to be drawn down to help pay for benefits and administrative expenses. The trustees project that the trust funds will continue to have a positive balance until 2033, allowing benefits scheduled under current law to be paid in full until that time.[7] After the trust funds are exhausted, which is projected to occur in 2033, the program would operate using current Social Security tax revenues, which would be sufficient to pay an estimated 75% of benefit payments scheduled under current law in 2033 and an estimated 73% of scheduled benefits in 2086. (See **Table 2** and **Figure 1**.)

In 2010, Social Security began operating with an annual cash flow deficit (i.e., income excluding interest is less than expenditures). The trustees project that Social Security will operate with an annual cash flow deficit in each year of the 75-year projection period (2012-2086). When Social Security operates with a cash flow deficit, the program cashes in federal government securities to supplement current Social Security tax revenues. General revenues are used to redeem the federal government securities held by the trust funds. When there are no surplus governmental receipts, the increased spending for Social Security from the general fund can only be paid for by the federal government raising taxes or other income, reducing other spending, or borrowing from the public (i.e., replacing bonds held by the trust funds with bonds held by the public). When total trust fund income (income including interest) is taken into account, the trustees project that Social Security will have a total surplus each year from 2012 to 2020.

Stated another way, the emergence of annual cash flow deficits means that the program begins to rely on interest credited to the trust funds to meet annual program costs (to help pay benefits and administrative expenses). Interest is credited to the trust funds in the form of new special issue securities; it does not represent a financial resource for the federal government from outside sources. As previously noted, general revenues are used to redeem the federal government securities held by the Social Security trust funds to cover the difference between Social Security tax revenues and program costs. In the 2012 trustees report, the trustees project that the program's reliance on general revenues will be $95.0 billion in 2020 (in constant 2012 dollars). The program's reliance on general revenues will increase as the trust fund balance begins to be drawn down (starting in 2021 when program costs exceed total income). For example, the program's reliance on general revenues is projected to be $318.7 billion in 2030 (in constant 2012 dollars). Projected *total* Social Security surpluses and deficits, as well as projected *cash flow* deficits, for each year from 2012 to 2032 are shown in **Table 2** and **Figure 2**.

With respect to the program's reliance on general revenues, it is important to note that the program is relying on revenues collected for Social Security purposes in previous years that were used by the federal government at the time for other (non-Social Security) spending needs. The Social Security program draws on those previously collected Social Security tax revenues (plus interest) when current Social Security tax revenues fall below current program expenditures.

---

[7] On a combined basis, the assets of the OASDI (Social Security) trust funds are projected to be exhausted in 2033. Separately, the OASI trust fund is projected to be exhausted in 2035, and the DI trust fund is projected to be exhausted in 2016. The trustees note " ... legislative action is needed as soon as possible. In the absence of a long-term solution, lawmakers could reallocate the payroll tax rate between OASI and DI, as they did in 1994." (2012 trustees report, p. 4.)

Table 1. Surplus Social Security Tax Revenues and Total Social Security Surplus, Calendar Years 1984 to 2009

(in millions of nominal dollars)

Calendar Year	Payroll Tax Revenues	Revenues from Taxation of Benefits[a]	Total Tax Revenues	Cost	Surplus Tax Revenues (Total Tax Revenues Minus Cost)	Total Surplus (Including Interest Income)
1984	$180,067	$3,025	$183,092	$180,429	$2,663	$6,208
1985	194,149	3,430	197,579	190,628	6,951	11,088
1986	209,140	3,662	212,802	201,522	11,280	4,698
1987	222,425	3,221	225,646	209,093	16,553	21,946
1988	251,814	3,445	255,259	222,514	32,745	40,955
1989	274,189	2,534	276,723	236,242	40,481	53,206
1990	296,070	4,992	301,062	253,135	47,927	62,309
1991	301,711	6,054	307,765	274,205	33,560	55,471
1992	311,128	6,084	317,212	291,865	25,347	50,726
1993	322,090	5,616	327,706	308,766	18,940	46,812
1994	344,695	5,306	350,001	323,011	26,990	58,100
1995	359,021	5,831	364,852	339,815	25,037	59,683
1996	378,881	6,844	385,725	353,569	32,156	70,883
1997	405,984	7,896	413,880	369,108	44,772	88,560
1998	430,174	9,707	439,881	382,255	57,626	106,950
1999	459,556	11,559	471,115	392,908	78,207	133,673
2000	492,484	12,314	504,798	415,121	89,677	153,312
2001	516,393	12,715	529,108	438,916	90,192	163,088
2002	532,471	13,839	546,310	461,653	84,657	165,432
2003	533,519	13,441	546,960	479,086	67,874	152,799
2004	553,040	15,703	568,743	501,643	67,100	156,075
2005	592,940	14,916	607,856	529,938	77,918	171,821
2006	625,594	16,858	642,452	555,421	87,031	189,452
2007	656,121	18,585	674,706	594,501	80,205	190,388
2008	672,122	16,879	689,001	625,143	63,858	180,159
2009	667,257	21,884	689,141	685,801	3,340	121,689

Source: Table prepared by CRS based on data from the Social Security Administration, http://www.ssa.gov/OACT/STATS/table4a3.html.

a. Some beneficiaries are required to pay federal income taxes on a portion of their benefits. For more information, see CRS Report RL32552, *Social Security: Calculation and History of Taxing Benefits.*

Table 2. Projected Income and Outgo of the Social Security Trust Funds, Under Intermediate Assumptions, Calendar Years 2012-2032

(in billions of constant 2012 dollars)

Year	Tax Revenues (or Non-Interest Income)	Interest Income	Total Income	Cost	Total Surplus/ Deficit[a]	Cash Flow Deficit[b]	Trust Fund Balance
2012	$735.5	$110.4	$846.0	$788.7	$57.3	-$53.2	$2,735.2
2013	750.9	105.9	856.8	816.5	40.3	-65.6	2,723.7
2014	783.0	104.4	887.4	846.6	40.8	-63.6	2,710.3
2015	814.8	104.4	919.2	878.6	40.6	-63.8	2,694.6
2016	847.7	105.1	952.8	910.2	42.6	-62.5	2,678.2
2017	880.9	106.1	987.0	942.4	44.6	-61.5	2,659.0
2018	912.0	107.7	1,019.7	976.8	42.9	-64.8	2,635.3
2019	934.4	108.9	1,043.3	1,011.8	31.5	-77.4	2,595.6
2020	955.1	109.4	1,064.5	1,050.1	14.4	-95.0	2,539.0
2021	973.8	108.6	1,082.5	1,088.9	-6.4	-115.1	2,463.4
2022	989.1	110.7	1,099.8	1,128.1	-28.3	-139.0	2,368.1
2023	1,004.8	111.6	1,116.4	1,168.7	-52.3	-163.9	2,251.3
2024	1,021.1	110.9	1,132.0	1,209.8	-77.8	-188.7	2,112.2
2025	1,037.8	108.5	1,146.3	1,250.6	-104.3	-212.8	1,950.3
2026	1,054.5	104.2	1,158.8	1,290.8	-132.0	-236.3	1,765.2
2027	1,071.3	93.2	1,164.5	1,330.8	-166.3	-259.5	1,550.8
2028	1,089.0	80.6	1,169.5	1,369.8	-200.3	-280.8	1,308.3
2029	1,106.6	66.4	1,173.0	1,407.0	-234.0	-300.4	1,038.6
2030	1,124.0	50.8	1,174.8	1,442.7	-267.9	-318.7	742.4
2031	1,142.1	33.7	1,175.7	1,477.0	-301.3	-334.9	421.0
2032[c]	1,161.2	15.2	1,176.4	1,510.0	-333.6	-348.8	75.9

Source: CRS, based on data from The 2012 Annual Report of the Board of Trustees of the Federal Old-Age and Survivors Insurance and Federal Disability Insurance Trust Funds, April 23, 2012, table VI.F7, available at http://www.socialsecurity.gov/OACT/TR/2012/lr6f7.html.

a. The total surplus/deficit for the year is equal to total income minus cost.

b. The *cash flow* deficit for the year is equal to tax revenues minus cost.

c. The Social Security trust funds are projected to be exhausted in 2033.

Figure 1. Projected Social Security Trust Fund Balances, Under the Intermediate Assumptions of the 2012 Trustees Report, Calendar Years 2012-2032

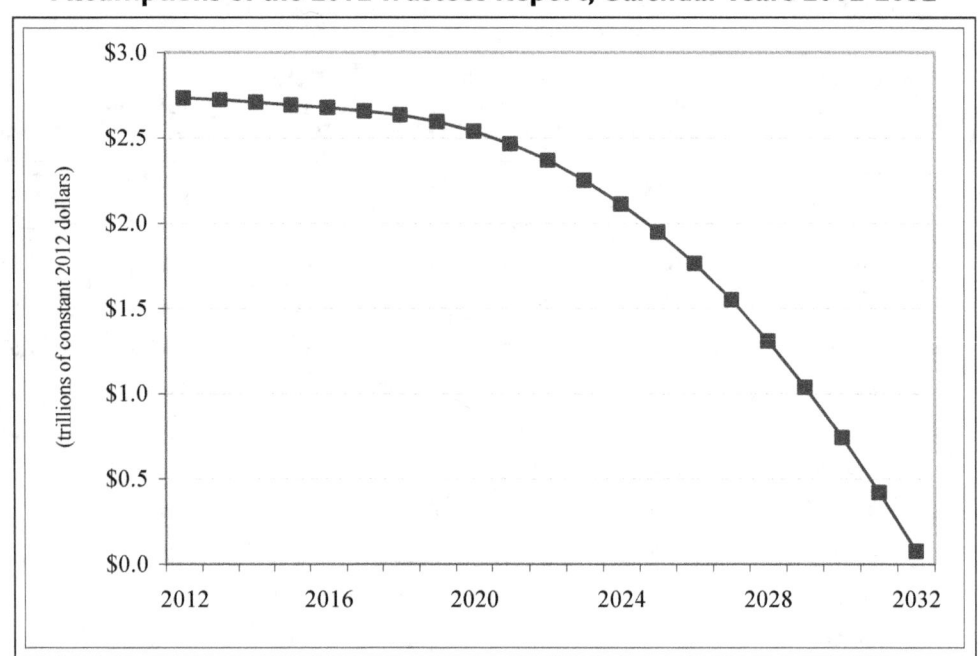

Figure 2. Projected Social Security Surpluses/Deficits, Under the Intermediate Assumptions of the 2012 Trustees Report, Calendar Years 2012-2032

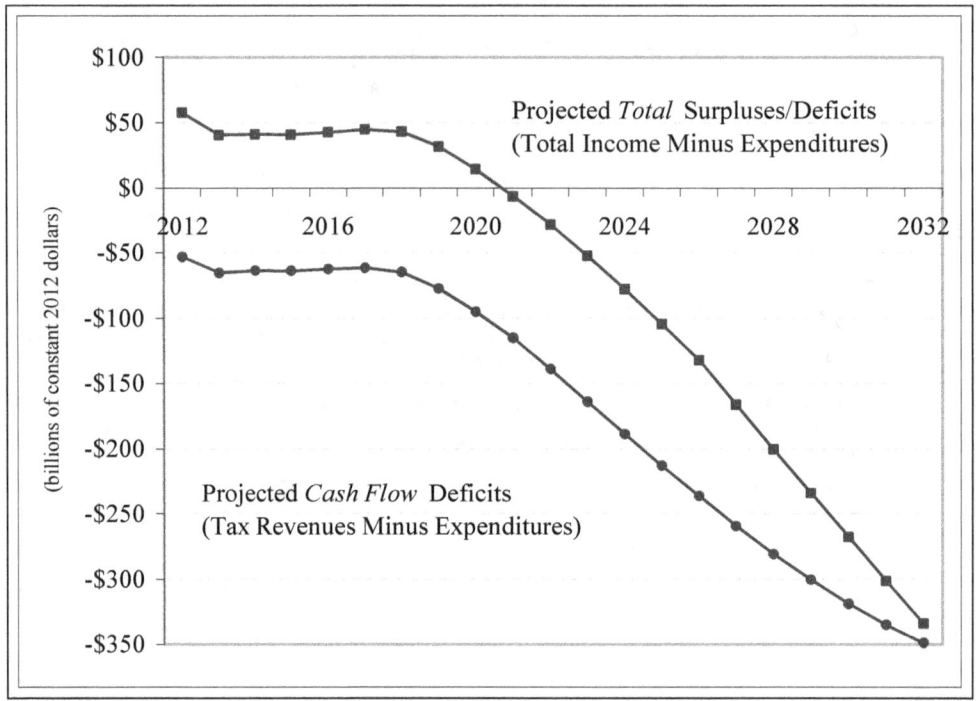

Source: Figures are based on data from The 2012 Annual Report of the Board of Trustees of the Federal Old-Age and Survivors Insurance and Federal Disability Insurance Trust Funds, April 23, 2012.

Social Security Trust Fund Solvency

The trustees project that the Social Security trust funds will be exhausted in 2033, at which point incoming receipts will cover an estimated 75% of scheduled annual benefits.[8] In addition, the trustees project that Social Security expenditures will exceed income by 19% on average over the next 75 years (2012-2086). Demographic changes are among the primary reasons for the system's projected funding shortfall. The first wave of the post-World War II baby boom generation began retiring in 2008, fertility rates continue to be lower than those experienced during the baby boom era (1946-1965), and life expectancy is projected to increase, factors that contribute to an older society. Between 2010 and 2030, the number of people aged 65 and older is projected to increase by 77%, whereas the number of workers whose taxes will finance future benefits is projected to increase by 7%. As a result, the number of workers supporting each Social Security beneficiary is projected to decline from 2.9 in 2011 to 2.0 in 2035.

In addition, program design features contribute to the projected growth in program spending. For example, elements of the Social Security benefit formula are indexed to average wage growth, resulting in a projected increase in the value of initial monthly benefits for future retirees. Wage indexing allows initial monthly benefits to replace a constant proportion of pre-retirement earnings for future retirees, so that initial monthly benefits keep pace with rising living standards.

Program Costs and Income as a Percentage of Taxable Payroll

The cost of the Social Security program in 2012 is estimated at $788.7 billion, an amount equal to 13.83% of workers' wages subject to the Social Security payroll tax (or taxable payroll).[9] The trustees project that program costs will increase to 17.41% of taxable payroll by 2035, decline to 17.07% in 2052, and then increase gradually to 17.83% in 2086.

By comparison, projections show relatively small increases in income rates over the period (annual income rates exclude interest income). As a percentage of taxable payroll, program income is projected to increase from 12.89% in 2012 to 13.33% in 2086. Income rates are projected to remain relatively stable over the period because the Social Security payroll tax rate (12.4% for employers and employees combined) is not scheduled to change under current law,[10]

---

[8] CBO projects that the Social Security trust funds will be exhausted in FY2034. On a separate basis, CBO projects that the OASI trust fund will be exhausted in 2038 and the DI trust fund will be exhausted in 2016. For more information, see *The 2012 Long-Term Projections for Social Security: Additional Information*, October 2012, http://www.cbo.gov/sites/default/files/cbofiles/attachments/43648-SocialSecurity.pdf. For CBO's near-term baseline estimates for the Social Security trust funds, see *Combined OASDI Trust Funds, March 2012 Baseline*, http://www.cbo.gov/sites/default/files/cbofiles/attachments/43063_Old-AgeSurvivorsDisabiityInsuranceTrustFunds.pdf. In the CBO table, the line labeled "Primary Surplus/Deficit" shows annual cash flows (excluding interest paid to the trust funds); the line labeled "Surplus/Deficit" shows annual totals including interest paid to the trust funds.

[9] Program costs and income are evaluated as a percentage of taxable payroll because Social Security payroll taxes are the primary source of funding for the program.

[10] Under current law, employers and employees each contribute 6.2% of covered earnings up to the taxable wage base ($110,100 in 2012). Self-employed workers contribute 12.4% of net self-employment income up to the taxable wage base. P.L. 111-312 (the Tax Relief, Unemployment Insurance Reauthorization, and Job Creation Act of 2010, signed by President Obama on December 17, 2010) provided a temporary 2 percentage point reduction in the payroll tax rate for employees and the self-employed in 2011. The Social Security payroll tax in 2011 was 4.2% for employees and 10.4% for the self-employed. P.L. 111-312 did not change the employer's share of the Social Security payroll tax (6.2%) or the taxable wage base ($106,800 in 2011). P.L. 111-312 provided general revenue transfers to the Social Security trust funds in amounts needed to protect the trust funds from the loss of payroll tax revenues. Similarly, P.L. 112-78 (the (continued...)

and income from the taxation of Social Security benefits is projected to increase only gradually relative to taxable payroll as the proportion of beneficiaries who must pay federal income taxes on a portion of their benefits increases gradually over time.[11] As a result, the gap between income and expenditures is projected to increase over the period. By 2086, program costs are projected to exceed income by 34% (or an amount equal to 4.50% of taxable payroll). On average, over the 75-year period (2012-2086), the cost of the program is projected to exceed income by 19% (or an amount equal to 2.67% of taxable payroll). (See **Table 3**.)

Table 3. Projected Social Security Income Rate, Cost Rate, and Balance as a Percentage of Taxable Payroll, Selected Calendar Years 2012-2086

(under the intermediate assumptions of the 2012 trustees report)

Year	Income Rate	Cost Rate	Balance
2012	12.89	13.83	-0.93
2015	12.95	13.97	-1.01
2020	13.07	14.37	-1.30
2025	13.18	15.88	-2.70
2030	13.25	17.01	-3.76
2035	13.28	17.41	-4.13
2040	13.28	17.36	-4.07
2045	13.28	17.19	-3.91
2050	13.27	17.08	-3.81
2055	13.28	17.09	-3.81
2060	13.28	17.16	-3.87
2065	13.29	17.20	-3.91
2070	13.30	17.33	-4.03
2075	13.31	17.46	-4.16
2080	13.32	17.60	-4.29
2085	13.33	17.79	-4.47
2086	13.33	17.83	-4.50
75 years: 2012-2086	14.02	16.69	-2.67

Source: The 2012 Annual Report of the Board of Trustees of the Federal Old-Age and Survivors Insurance and Federal Disability Insurance Trust Funds, April 23, 2012, table VI.F2 and table VI.F3.

Note: Annual income rates exclude interest income.

(...continued)

Temporary Payroll Tax Cut Continuation Act of 2011, signed by President Obama on December 23, 2011) extended the payroll tax reduction for workers through February 2012. P.L. 112-96 (the Middle Class Tax Relief and Job Creation Act of 2012, signed by President Obama on February 22, 2012) further extended the payroll tax reduction for workers through December 2012. The Social Security payroll tax rate for workers in effect through December 2012 is 4.2% (rather than 6.2%). For more information, see CRS Report R41648, *Social Security: Temporary Payroll Tax Reduction*, by Dawn Nuschler.

[11] For more information on the taxation of Social Security benefits, see CRS Report RL32552, *Social Security: Calculation and History of Taxing Benefits*, by Christine Scott.

Program Costs and Income as a Percentage of Gross Domestic Product

Social Security program costs and income are also evaluated as a share of U.S. economic output. The cost of the program is projected to increase gradually from 5.01% of gross domestic product (GDP) in 2012 to 6.36% of GDP in 2035, before declining to 6.12% of GDP by 2050 and then remaining at about that level.

By comparison, program income as a percentage of GDP is projected to remain relatively stable over the period (annual income excludes interest income). Program income is projected to increase from 4.67% of GDP in 2012 to 4.91% in 2021. Program income as a percentage of GDP is then projected to decline gradually to 4.83% in 2040 and 4.56% in 2085. Program income is projected to decline as a share of GDP because wages subject to the Social Security payroll tax are projected to increase more slowly than other forms of employee compensation and other types of income. In 2085, the projected funding shortfall is an amount equal to 1.53% of GDP. On average, over the 75-year period (2012-2086), the projected funding shortfall is an amount equal to 0.96% of GDP. (See **Table 4.**)

Table 4. Projected Social Security Income, Cost, and Balance as a Percentage of Gross Domestic Product (GDP), Selected Calendar Years 2012-2086

(under the intermediate assumptions of the 2012 trustees report)

Year	Income	Cost	Balance
2012	4.67	5.01	-0.34
2015	4.73	5.10	-0.37
2020	4.89	5.38	-0.49
2025	4.89	5.89	-1.00
2030	4.87	6.25	-1.38
2035	4.85	6.36	-1.51
2040	4.83	6.31	-1.48
2045	4.79	6.21	-1.41
2050	4.76	6.12	-1.36
2055	4.73	6.08	-1.36
2060	4.69	6.06	-1.37
2065	4.66	6.04	-1.37
2070	4.63	6.04	-1.40
2075	4.61	6.04	-1.44
2080	4.58	6.06	-1.48
2085	4.56	6.09	-1.53
2086	4.56	6.10	-1.54
75 years: 2012-2086	5.05	6.01	-0.96

Source: The 2012 Annual Report of the Board of Trustees of the Federal Old-Age and Survivors Insurance and Federal Disability Insurance Trust Funds, April 23, 2012, table VI.F4, pp. 197-198, and online at http://www.socialsecurity.gov/OACT/TR/2012/lr6f4.html. Income for individual years excludes interest on the trust funds. Interest is implicit in the summarized value.

The projected long-range financial outlook for the Social Security system is reflected in public opinion polls that show less than 50% of respondents are confident in Social Security's ability to meet its long-term commitments.[12] There is a growing public perception that Social Security may not be as good a value in the future. Until recent years, retirees could expect to receive more in benefits than they paid in Social Security payroll taxes. However, because Social Security payroll tax rates have increased to cover the costs of the maturing "pay-as-you-go" system, these ratios have become less favorable. Such concerns, and a belief that the nation must increase national savings to meet the needs of an aging society, are among the factors behind reform efforts.

Supporters of the current program structure suggest that the issues confronting the system are not as serious as sometimes portrayed and believe there is no imminent crisis. They point out that the trust funds are projected to have a balance until 2033, there continues to be public support for the program, and there would be considerable risk in some of the reform ideas. They contend that relatively modest changes could restore long-range solvency to the system.[13]

Basic Debate

The Social Security system has faced funding shortfalls in the past. In 1977 and 1983, Congress enacted a variety of measures to address the system's financial imbalance. These measures include constraints on the growth of initial benefit levels, a gradual increase in the full retirement age from 65 to 67 (i.e., the age at which unreduced benefits are first payable), payroll tax increases, taxation of benefits for higher-income beneficiaries, and extension of Social Security coverage to federal and nonprofit workers. Subsequently, projections showed the re-emergence of long-term deficits as a result of changes in actuarial methods and assumptions, and because program changes had been evaluated with respect to their effect on the *average* 75-year deficit. That is, while program changes were projected to restore trust fund solvency on average over the 75-year period, a period of surpluses was followed by a period of deficits.

Many policymakers believe that some type of action should be taken sooner rather than later. This view has been shared by the Social Security trustees and other panels and commissions that have examined the issue. In recent years, a wide range of interest groups have echoed this view in testimony before Congress. However, there is no consensus on whether the projections represent a "crisis." In 1977 and 1983, the trust fund balances were projected to fall to zero within a very short period (within months of the 1983 reforms). Today, the problem is perceived to be as many as 22 years away (based on the projected trust fund exhaustion date). Lacking a "crisis," the pressure to compromise is diffused and the issues and the divergent views about them have led to myriad complex proposals. In 1977 and 1983, the debate was not about fundamental reform. Rather, it revolved around how to raise the system's income and constrain costs. Today, the ideas range from restoring the system's solvency with as few alterations as possible to replacing it entirely with something modeled after IRAs or 401(k)s. This broad spectrum was reflected in the 1997 Social Security Advisory Council report, which presented three different reform plans. None of the plans was supported by a majority of the 13-member council. Similar diversity is reflected in the Social Security reform bills introduced in recent Congresses.

---

[12] Polling results are from PollingReport.com at http://www.pollingreport.com/social.htm (see ABC News/Washington Post Poll, February 19-22, 2009).

[13] For more information on Social Security trust fund operations, see CRS Report RL33028, *Social Security: The Trust Fund*, by Dawn Nuschler and Gary Sidor.

Push for Major Reform

Advocates of reform view Social Security as an anachronism, built on depression-era concerns about high unemployment and widespread "dependency" among the aged. They see the prospect of reform today as an opportunity to "modernize" the way society saves for retirement. They maintain that the vast economic, social and demographic changes that have transpired over the past 75 years require the system to change, and they point to changes made in other countries that now use market-based individual accounts to strengthen retirement incomes and bolster their economies by spurring savings and investments. They believe government-run, pay-as-you-go systems are unsustainable in aging societies. They prefer a system that allows workers to acquire wealth and provide for their retirement by investing in individual accounts.

Reform advocates also view it as a way to counter skepticism about the current system by giving workers a greater sense of "ownership" of their retirement savings. They contend that private investments would yield larger retirement incomes because stocks and bonds historically have provided higher returns than are projected from the current system. Some believe that individual accounts would address what they view as the system's contradictory mix of insurance and social welfare goals. Others maintain that creating a system of individual accounts would prevent the government from using any surplus Social Security tax revenues for other government spending. Recent stock market declines and the emergence of annual cash flow deficits for the Social Security system, however, have made investment-based proposals less popular among some policymakers in the near term.

Some, who do not necessarily seek a new system, view enactment of long-range Social Security constraints as one way to curb federal entitlement spending. The aging of society means that the cost of entitlement programs that aid the elderly will increase greatly in the future. The costs of the largest entitlement programs (Social Security, Medicare, and Medicaid) are directly linked to an aging population. Proponents of imposing constraints on these programs express concern that, if left unchecked, their costs will place pressure on the federal budget far into the future, consuming resources that could be used for other priorities and forcing future generations to bear a much higher tax burden.

As a matter of fairness, it has been pointed out that many current beneficiaries get back more than the value of their Social Security contributions, and far more than the baby boom generation will receive. They believe that to delay making changes to the program is unfair to current workers, who must pay for "transfer" payments that they characterize as "overgenerous" and unrelated to need, while facing the prospect that their own benefits may have to be scaled back severely. Others emphasize the system's projected long-range funding shortfall and contend that steps should be taken soon (e.g., raising the retirement age, restraining the growth of initial monthly benefits for future retirees, reducing cost-of-living adjustments, increasing the taxable wage base) so that changes can be phased-in, allowing workers more time to adjust their retirement expectations and plans to reflect what the program will be able to provide in the future. They maintain that more abrupt changes in taxes and benefits would otherwise be required.

Arguments for Retaining the Existing System

Those who favor a more restrained approach believe that the issues facing the system can be resolved with modest tax and spending changes, and that the program's critics are raising the specter that Social Security will "bankrupt the nation" to undermine public support and provide an excuse to incorporate individual accounts into the system. They contend that individual savings accounts would erode the social insurance nature of the program, which favors low-wage workers, the disabled, and survivors.

Others are concerned that switching to a new system of individual accounts would pose large transition problems by requiring younger workers to save for their own retirement while paying taxes to cover benefits for current retirees. Some doubt that it would increase national savings, arguing that higher government debt (resulting from the redirection of current payroll taxes to individual accounts) would offset the increased individual account savings. They also contend that the capital markets' inflow created by the accounts would make the markets difficult to regulate and potentially distort equity valuations. They point out that some of the countries that have moved to individual accounts did so to create capital markets. Such markets, they argue, are already well developed in the United States.

Some believe that a system of individual accounts would expose participants to excessive market risk for an income source that has become essential to many of the nation's elderly. They say that the nation has a three-tiered retirement system (Social Security, private pensions, and personal assets) that already includes private savings and investment. They contend that while people may be willing and able to undertake some "risk" in the latter two tiers, Social Security (as the tier that provides a basic floor of protection) should be more stable. They further contend that the administrative costs of maintaining individual accounts could be very large and erode the value of the accounts.

Specific Areas of Contention

System's Financial Outlook

There are conflicting views about the severity of Social Security's projected funding shortfall. Some maintain that the problem is more acute than portrayed under the traditional 75-year projections that show an average 75-year deficit equal to 2.67% of taxable payroll ($8.6 trillion in present value terms). They believe this view is supported by an alternative portrayal in the trustees' report that extends the projections indefinitely into the future. On an "infinite horizon" basis, the projected funding shortfall is equal to 3.9% of taxable payroll ($20.5 trillion in present value terms). They also point out that, in 2030 for example, the cost of the system is projected to exceed income by an amount equal to 3.76% of taxable payroll (costs are projected to exceed income by 28%). By the end of the projection period (2086), however, the cost of the system is projected to exceed income by an amount equal to 4.50% of taxable payroll (costs are projected to exceed income by 34%). On a *pay-as-you-go basis*, the system would require more than a 19% change in taxes or expenditures over the next 75 years to cover projected program costs (over the next 75 years, *on average*, the cost of the system is projected to exceed income by 19%). In addition, they point out that the current 75-year actuarial deficit projected for the trust funds (2.67% of taxable payroll) is the largest actuarial deficit reported since prior to the 1983 Social Security Amendments, and the largest single-year worsening of the actuarial deficit since the 1994 Trustees Report.

They maintain that viewing the problem as 22 years away (because the trust funds are projected to have a positive balance until 2033) does not take into account the pressure Social Security will exert on the federal budget in the coming years as annual cash flow deficits require the system to rely on assets held by the trust funds (federal government securities) to meet annual expenditures. The federal government securities held by the trust funds are redeemed with general revenues. Therefore, the government must rely on other financial resources to help pay Social Security benefits and administrative expenses, resources that could be used to finance other governmental functions.

Others maintain that, in contrast to earlier episodes of financial imbalance, the system has no "immediate" problem: the trust funds are projected to have a positive balance until 2033 and can pay benefits scheduled under current law (in full and on time) until then. For this reason, they maintain that policymakers have time to address changes to the Social Security program. They point out that there is inherent uncertainty surrounding the trust fund projections over a 75-year period, let alone the infinite horizon. Even if the 75-year projections hold, they point out, for example, that the average imbalance could be eliminated by increasing the combined employer and employee payroll tax rate during the period in a manner equivalent to an immediate increase of 2.61 percentage points (from the current level of 12.40% to 15.01%).

While acknowledging that the cost of the system is projected to represent a notably larger share of GDP in the future (increasing from 5.01% of GDP today to 6.36% of GDP in 2035), they point out that GDP itself would have risen substantially in real terms. Moreover, while the ratio of workers to beneficiaries is projected to decline, they believe that employers are likely to respond with inducements for older workers to stay on the job longer. Phased retirements are becoming more prevalent, and some older workers view retirement as more than an all-or-nothing decision. In addition, they argue that Social Security program changes should not be considered in the context of broader deficit reduction efforts as policymakers look for ways to restrain federal budget deficits; rather, Social Security program changes should be considered separately.

Public Confidence

In recent years, public opinion polls have shown that a majority of Americans lack confidence in the system's ability to meet its future commitments. Younger workers are particularly skeptical. For example, in one recent poll of non-retired adults aged 18 or older, 70% of those in the 18-49 age group said they did not think the Social Security system would be able to pay them a benefit when they retire, compared with 34% in the 50 or older age group.[14]

Some observers express caution about inferring too much from polling data, arguing that public understanding of Social Security is limited and often inaccurate. They maintain that a major reason confidence is highest among older persons is that they have learned more about Social Security because they are more immediately affected by the program. Some believe that the annual Social Security Statements provided by the Social Security Administration (SSA) will make workers more aware of their estimated future benefits scheduled under current law and thus more trusting of the system.[15] Others suggest, however, that the skepticism is justified by the system's repeated financial difficulties and diminished "money's worth" for younger workers.

---

[14] Polling results are from PollingReport.com at http://www.pollingreport.com/social.htm (see CNN/Opinion Research Corporation Poll, August 6-10, 2010).

[15] In 2012, SSA made the annual Social Security Statement available online. For more information, go to http://www.ssa.gov/mystatement/.

Doubts About Money's Worth

Until recent years, Social Security beneficiaries received more, often far more, than the value of the Social Security taxes they paid. However, because Social Security payroll tax rates have increased over the years and the full retirement age (the age at which unreduced benefits are first payable) is being increased gradually, it is becoming more apparent that Social Security will be less of a good deal for many future retirees. For example, for workers who earned average wages and retired in 1980 at the age of 65, it took 2.8 years to recover the value of the retirement portion of the combined employee and employer shares of their Social Security taxes plus interest. For their counterparts who retired at the age of 65 in 2003, it will take 17.4 years. For those retiring in 2020, it will take 21.6 years. Some observers believe these discrepancies are inequitable and cite them as evidence that the system needs to be substantially restructured.

Others discount this phenomenon, viewing Social Security as a *social insurance* program serving social ends that transcend questions of whether some individuals fare better than others. For example, the program's anti-poverty features are designed to replace a higher proportion of earnings for lower-wage workers and provide additional benefits for workers with families. Some observers point out that current workers, who will receive less direct value from their taxes compared with current retirees, have in part been relieved from having to support their parents, and many elderly are able to live independently and with dignity. These observers contend that the value of these aspects of the program is not reflected in comparisons of taxes and benefits.

Debate Over Individual Accounts

Social Security's projected long-range financial outlook, skepticism about the sustainability of the current system, and a belief that economic growth could be bolstered through increased savings have led to a number of proposals to incorporate individual accounts into the Social Security system, reviving a debate that dates back to the creation of the program in 1935. All three plans presented by the 1994-1996 Social Security Advisory Council featured program involvement in the financial markets. The first called upon Congress to consider authorizing investment of part of the Social Security trust funds in equities (on the assumption that stocks would produce a higher return to the system). The second would require workers to contribute an extra 1.6% of pay to individual accounts to make up for Social Security benefit reductions called for under the plan to restore the system's long-range solvency. The third would redesign the system by gradually replacing Social Security retirement benefits with flat-rate benefits based on length of service and individual accounts (funded with 5 percentage points of the current Social Security tax rate).[16]

The reform that Chile enacted in 1981, which replaced a troubled pay-as-you-go system with one requiring workers to invest part of their earnings in individual accounts through government-approved pension funds, has been reflected in a number of reform bills introduced in recent Congresses.[17] These measures would permit or require workers to invest some or all of their Social Security payroll taxes in individual accounts. Most call for future Social Security benefits to be reduced or forfeited. Similarly, the three options presented by the Social Security reform

---

[16] *Report of the 1994-1996 Advisory Council on Social Security, Volume I: Findings and Recommendations,* Washington, DC, January 1997.

[17] For more information on the pension system in Chile, see CRS Report R42449, *Chile's Pension System: Background in Brief,* by Alison M. Shelton.

commission appointed by former President Bush in 2001 would allow workers to participate in individual accounts and would reduce their future Social Security benefit by the projected value of the account based on an assumed (rather than the actual) rate of return.[18]

Another approach is reflected in bills that would require any budget surpluses to be used to finance individual accounts to supplement Social Security benefits for those who pay Social Security payroll taxes. Former President Clinton's January 1999 reform plan would have allocated a portion of budget surpluses to individual accounts, supplemented by a worker's own contributions and a government match (scaled to income). In addition, the plan would have redirected a portion of budget surpluses, or the interest savings resulting therefrom, to the Social Security trust funds. Some of the funds would have been used to acquire stocks, similar to the approach suggested in one of the Advisory Council plans and some past legislation. Most of these approaches would require establishment of an independent board to invest some of the funds in stocks or corporate bonds and the remaining funds in federal securities.

Some individual account proponents believe that individual accounts would reduce future financial demands on government and reassure workers by giving them a sense of "ownership" of their retirement savings. Others believe that individual accounts would enhance workers' retirement income because stocks and bonds generally have provided higher rates of return than are projected from Social Security. In conjunction with this, they maintain that individual accounts would increase national savings and promote economic growth. Others maintain that individual accounts would prevent the government from using any surplus Social Security revenues to "mask" public borrowing, or for other spending or tax reductions. Generally, proponents of an individual account system express concern that "collective" investment of the Social Security trust funds in the markets would concentrate too much economic power in a government-appointed board.[19]

Opponents of individual accounts maintain that Social Security's projected long-range funding shortfall could be resolved without altering the fundamental nature of the program. They express concern that replacing Social Security with individual accounts would erode the social insurance aspects of the system that favor lower-wage workers, survivors and the disabled. Others are concerned that individual accounts would pose large transition problems by requiring younger workers to save for their own retirement while simultaneously paying taxes to support current beneficiaries, and would further exacerbate current budget deficits. Some doubt that individual accounts would increase national savings, maintaining that any increase in private savings would be offset by increased government borrowing. They also point out that the investment pool created by the accounts could be difficult to regulate and distort capital markets and equity valuations. Still others view it as exposing participants to excessive market risk for something as essential as core retirement benefits and, unlike Social Security, as providing poor protection against inflation. Many prefer "collective" investment of the Social Security trust funds in the markets to potentially bolster their returns and spread the risks of poor performance broadly.

---

[18] *Strengthening Social Security and Creating Personal Wealth for All Americans*, Final Report of the President's Commission to Strengthen Social Security, December 21, 2001.

[19] For examples of arguments in support of individual accounts, see *Strengthening Social Security and Creating Personal Wealth for All Americans*, Final Report of the President's Commission to Strengthen Social Security, December 21, 2001, and a variety of sources available from the Cato Institute at http://www.socialsecurity.org/.

Maximum Taxable Earnings Base

Social Security payroll taxes are levied on Social Security-covered earnings up to a maximum amount set each year. In 2013, this maximum amount—which is referred to as the *contribution and benefit base* or the *taxable earnings base*—is $113,700. The taxable earnings base is adjusted each year based on average wage growth, if a Social Security cost-of-living adjustment (COLA) is payable. The taxable earnings base limits the amount of annual wages or self-employment income used to determine a worker's contributions to Social Security.[20] It also limits the amount of annual wages or self-employment income used to compute a worker's benefit, and thus sets a ceiling on the amount of a worker's initial monthly benefit.

Under current law, a small percentage of workers have earnings *at or above* the taxable earnings base. In 2009, for example, an estimated 5.4% of workers had earnings *at or above* the taxable earnings base of $106,800 that year.[21]

Supporters of raising or eliminating the taxable earnings base point out that it could reduce or eliminate Social Security's projected long-range funding shortfall. The full impact of the policy change would depend on how the proposal is structured and whether the additional taxable earnings are counted for benefit computation purposes.

Raising or eliminating the taxable earnings base for both contribution and benefit purposes would result in an increase in payroll tax revenues, as well as an increase in benefit payments to some beneficiaries. Higher benefit payments would increase program spending, however, the increase in expenditures would be more than offset by the increase in tax revenues. Some observers express concern about the potential level of initial monthly benefits that would be payable to some beneficiaries, particularly under a scenario in which all covered earnings would be taxable and counted for benefit computation purposes. The trust fund solvency impact of the policy change would be greater if the limit on taxable earnings were raised or eliminated for contribution purposes only (i.e., if the additional taxable earnings were not counted for benefit computation purposes). This approach, however, raises concerns of equity among some because it would break the traditional link between contributions and benefits and could potentially weaken support for the program among higher-wage workers.

Some observers maintain that the taxable earnings base should cover a steady percentage of Social Security-covered earnings. The percentage of *covered workers* with earnings below the taxable earnings base has remained relatively stable at about 94% since the 1980s. In comparison, however, the percentage of *covered earnings* subject to the payroll tax has declined over the period, from 90% in 1982 to an estimated 84% in 2010.[22] Generally, the decline in the percentage of covered earnings that are taxable is attributed in large part to relatively faster wage growth for

---

[20] Under permanent law, employers and employees each contribute 6.2% of an employee's covered earnings up to the annual taxable limit, and self-employed workers contribute 12.4% of net self-employment income up to the annual taxable limit. Some workers (approximately 6%) are not covered under the Social Security program and therefore do not pay Social Security payroll taxes.

[21] Social Security Administration, *Annual Statistical Supplement, 2011*, Table 4.B4, available at http://www.socialsecurity.gov/policy/docs/statcomps/supplement/2011/4b.pdf.

[22] Social Security Administration, *Annual Statistical Supplement, 2011*, Table 4.B4 and Table 4.B1, available at http://www.socialsecurity.gov/policy/docs/statcomps/supplement/2011/4b.pdf. The Social Security Amendments of 1977 (P.L. 95-216) increased the taxable earnings base to a level that would make 90% of aggregate earnings in covered employment taxable by 1982, as a revenue raising measure.

---

high earners, compared to workers with wages below the taxable earnings base. The Social Security trustees project that the percentage of covered earnings subject to the payroll tax will be about 83% in 2021.[23]

Some policymakers have proposed raising the taxable earnings base to a level that would make 90% of aggregate covered earnings subject to the payroll tax, as Congress did in 1977. This proposal has been reflected in the recommendations of recent deficit reduction commissions, including the 2010 National Commission on Fiscal Responsibility and Reform (the President's Fiscal Commission). Among the changes proposed for Social Security, the commission recommended a gradual increase in the taxable wage base such that 90% of aggregate wages in covered employment would be taxable by 2050.[24] The Social Security Administration estimates that an increase in the taxable earnings base such that 90% of earnings would be subject to the payroll tax (phased in from 2012 to 2021) would improve the system's projected long-range actuarial balance by 36% if the additional taxable earnings are credited for benefit computation purposes, and by 45% if the additional taxable earnings are not credited.[25]

Some critics of this approach argue that it would disproportionately affect those with earnings just above the current taxable earnings base relative to those with very high earnings. Therefore, proposals to increase the amount of wages subject to the Social Security payroll tax take different forms. For example, some proposals would (1) maintain the Social Security payroll tax on covered earnings up to the current-law taxable earnings base, and (2) make covered earnings above a second higher threshold (such as $250,000) subject to the Social Security payroll tax.[26] Still other proposals would require workers and employers each to pay an additional tax (such as 3%) on covered earnings above the current-law taxable earnings base (in addition to the 6.2% each on covered earnings up to the taxable earnings base payable under current law).[27]

Retirement Age Issue

Raising the Social Security retirement age is often considered as a way to help restore long-range solvency to the system. Some of the projected growth in Social Security's costs is a result of projected increases in life expectancy (and, as a result, more years spent in retirement). Since benefits were first paid in 1940, life expectancy at age 65 has increased from 12.7 years for men and 14.7 years for women to 18.7 years for men and 20.7 years for women. By 2030, life expectancy at age 65 is projected to reach 20.0 years for men and 21.9 years for women.[28]

This trend bolstered arguments for increasing the full retirement age (FRA, the age at which unreduced retirement benefits are first payable) as a way to achieve savings when the system was facing major financial problems in the early 1980s. As part of the Social Security Amendments of

---

[23] 2012 trustees report, intermediate assumptions, p. 136.

[24] More information on the Social Security recommendations of the President's Fiscal Commission is provided in a later section of this report.

[25] Social Security Administration, Office of the Chief Actuary, *Provisions Affecting Payroll Tax Rates*, available at http://www.ssa.gov/OACT/solvency/provisions/payrolltax.html (see options E3.1 and E3.2, respectively). Estimates are based on the intermediate assumptions of the 2011 trustees report.

[26] For example, see H.R. 797 and S. 1558 introduced in the 112th Congress (described in a later section of this report).

[27] For example, see H.R. 1863 introduced in the 111th Congress (described in a later section of this report).

[28] Projections of cohort life expectancy are based on the intermediate assumptions of the 2012 trustees report (see table V.A4, p. 91).

1983 (P.L. 98-21), Congress raised the FRA from 65 to 67. The increase in the FRA enacted in 1983 is currently being phased-in starting with persons born in 1938, with the full two-year increase affecting persons born in 1960 or later.[29] The 1983 amendments did not raise the early retirement age (age 62). However, the benefit reduction for persons who retire at age 62 will increase from 20% to 30%. Proponents of increasing the early or full retirement age view it as reasonable in light of projected increases in life expectancy. Opponents believe it would penalize workers who already get a worse deal from Social Security compared to current retirees, persons who work in physically demanding occupations, and racial minorities and others who have shorter life expectancies.

Cost-of-Living Adjustments

Social Security benefits are adjusted annually to reflect inflation as measured by the Bureau of Labor Statistics' (BLS's) Consumer Price Index (CPI), which measures price increases for selected goods and services.[30] The CPI has been criticized for overstating the effects of inflation, primarily because the index's market basket of goods and services was not revised regularly to reflect changes in consumer buying habits or improvements in quality. A BLS analysis in 1993 found that the annual overstatement may be as much as 0.6 percentage point. CBO estimated in 1994 that the overstatement ranged from 0.2 to 0.8 percentage point. A 1996 panel that studied the issue for the Senate Finance Committee argued that it may be 1.1 percentage points.[31] In response to its own analysis as well as outside criticisms, the BLS has since made various revisions to the CPI. To some extent, these revisions may account for part of the slower CPI growth in recent years. However, calls for adjustments continue.[32]

In August 2002, BLS introduced a supplemental index—the chained CPI-U (C-CPI-U). The goal of the C-CPI-U is to more accurately reflect how consumers change their buying habits in response to price changes.[33] Some policymakers support using the C-CPI-U to compute the annual Social Security cost-of-living adjustment (COLA) on the basis that other CPI measures (including the CPI-W) overestimate how much money is needed to maintain a constant standard of living.[34] Although some view using a different measure of price change to adjust benefits for inflation as a necessary way to help keep Social Security and other entitlement spending under control, others view such changes as a backdoor way of reducing benefits. They maintain that the market basket of goods and services purchased by the elderly is different from that of the general population around which the CPI is constructed. It is more heavily weighted with healthcare expenditures, which rise notably faster than the overall CPI, and thus they contend that the cost of

---

[29] For more information, see CRS Report R41962, *Fact Sheet: The Social Security Retirement Age*, by Alison M. Shelton.

[30] Under current law, the CPI measure used to adjust Social Security benefits is the Consumer Price Index for Urban Wage Earners and Clerical Workers (CPI-W).

[31] *Toward a More Accurate Measure of the Cost of Living*, Final Report to the Senate Finance Committee from the Advisory Commission to Study the Consumer Price Index, December 4, 1996.

[32] For more information, see CRS Report RL30074, *The Consumer Price Index: A Brief Overview*, by Brian W. Cashell, and CRS Report RL34168, *Automatic Cost of Living Adjustments: Some Economic and Practical Considerations*, by Brian W. Cashell.

[33] For more information, see CRS Report RL32293, *The Chained Consumer Price Index: What Is It and Would It Be Appropriate for Cost-of-Living Adjustments?*, by Linda Levine.

[34] For more information, see CRS Report R42086, *Using a Different Cost-of-Living Measure for Social Security Beneficiaries: Some Policy Considerations*, by Alison M. Shelton.

living for the elderly is higher than reflected by the CPI. For this reason, some policymakers support using the Consumer Price Index for the Elderly (CPI-E), an experimental index developed by BLS, to compute the annual Social Security COLA.[35]

According to the Social Security Administration, a reduction in the Social Security COLA of 0.5 percentage point annually (beginning December 2012) would improve the system's projected long-range actuarial balance by 38%. Similarly, a COLA reduction of 1 percentage point annually would improve the system's projected long-range actuarial balance by 74%.[36]

Social Security and the Budget

By law, Social Security is considered "off budget" for many aspects of developing and enforcing annual budget goals. However, it is a federal program and its income and outgo help shape the year-to-year financial condition of the federal government. As a result, policymakers often focus on "unified" (or overall) budget totals that include Social Security. When former President Clinton urged that the unified budget surpluses projected at the time be reserved until Social Security's projected long-range funding issues were resolved, and proposed using a portion of those surpluses to shore up the system, Social Security's budget treatment became a major issue. Congressional views about what to do with the surpluses were diverse, ranging from "buying down" publicly held federal debt to cutting taxes to increasing spending. However, there was substantial support for setting aside a portion equal to the annual Social Security trust fund surpluses.

After budget deficits re-emerged, there continued to be some congressional interest in the concept of a Social Security "lock box." For example, in the 109th Congress, H.R. 3435 (Savings for Seniors Act of 2005 introduced by Representative Blackburn) would have established a Social Security Surplus Protection Account in the OASI trust fund for the purpose of "holding" surplus Social Security tax revenues. It would have established a Social Security Investment Commission to recommend alternative investment options for surplus Social Security funds. Under the measure, investment of funds held in the account would have been suspended pending enactment of legislation providing for trust fund investment in nongovernmental assets. Also in the 109th Congress, S. 1730 (Truth in Budgeting Act of 2005 introduced by Senator Voinovich) would have established a Trust Fund Administration within the Treasury Department for the purpose of investing all federal trust fund revenues in nongovernmental debt instruments (such as municipal and corporate bonds) upon the issuance of special rate Treasury obligations to the trust funds (investment in stocks would have been prohibited). Under the measure, investment fund assets would have been used to redeem outstanding special rate Treasury obligations.

In the 109th Congress, Senator DeMint offered an amendment to the Senate budget resolution for FY2007 (S.Con.Res. 83) that would have allowed for the creation of a reserve fund for surplus

---

[35] For information on the CPI-E, see CRS Report RS20060, *A Separate Consumer Price Index for the Elderly?*, by Linda Levine. For information on the projected effects of using the C-CPI-U and the CPI-E to compute the annual Social Security COLA, see Social Security Administration, Office of the Chief Actuary, Memo to the Honorable Xavier Becerra, June 21, 2011, available at http://ssa.gov/OACT/solvency/index.html.

[36] Social Security Administration, Office of the Chief Actuary, *Provisions Affecting Cost of Living Adjustment*, available at http://www.ssa.gov/OACT/solvency/provisions/cola.html (see options A2 and A1, respectively). Estimates are based on the intermediate assumptions of the 2011 trustees report. In the 2011 trustees report, the projected 75-year actuarial deficit for the Social Security trust funds was 2.22% of taxable payroll. The percentages shown here (38% and 74%) are derived from the SSA information as follows: (1) 0.85% / 2.22% = 38% and (2) 1.64% / 2.22% = 74%.

Social Security tax revenues, provided that the Senate Finance Committee approve Social Security legislation that meets certain requirements. For example, the amendment (S.Amdt. 3087) specified that such legislation make no changes to Social Security benefits scheduled under current law for individuals born before 1950 and provide individuals with "the option to voluntarily obtain legally binding ownership of at least some portion of each participant's benefits." The amendment was defeated by a vote of 46-53.

In the 110th Congress, the FY2008 budget resolution (S.Con.Res. 21) passed by the Senate on March 23, 2007, included provisions aimed at "protecting" annual Social Security surpluses. The Senate-passed version of the budget resolution included a provision that would have created a new "Point of Order to Save Social Security First." The provision would have allowed a floor objection to be raised in the Senate against consideration of any legislation that would increase the *on-budget* deficit in any fiscal year (i.e., a deficit in the part of the federal budget that excludes Social Security and the Postal Service). The point of order could be raised against such legislation until the President submits legislation to Congress, and Congress enacts legislation, that would restore long-range solvency to the Social Security system (as scored by the Social Security Administration). The point of order could be waived with a three-fifths majority vote in the Senate. The Senate-passed version also included a provision ("Circuit Breaker to Protect Social Security") that would have provided a point of order against any budget resolution that does not achieve an *on-budget* balance within five years, with exceptions provided for periods of war or low economic growth. The point of order could be waived with a three-fifths majority vote in the Senate. These provisions, however, were not included in the FY2008 budget resolution conference report (S.Con.Res. 21, H.Rept. 110-153) passed by the House and Senate on May 17, 2007.[37]

Today, some policymakers support Social Security program changes as a way to reduce federal entitlement spending and federal budget deficits. Some policymakers who support efforts to restrain the growth in major entitlement programs such as Social Security, Medicare, and Medicaid express concern that federal spending for these programs is contributing to unsustainable levels of federal budget deficits that have a negative impact on the economy. Policymakers differ as to how to restrain spending growth for these programs. With respect to Social Security, policymakers differ in particular as to how to apportion benefit reductions and tax increases between workers and retirees in the future.

On February 18, 2010, President Obama established by executive order the National Commission on Fiscal Responsibility and Reform. The executive order states "the Commission shall propose recommendations that meaningfully improve the long-run fiscal outlook, including changes to address the growth of entitlement spending and the gap between the projected revenues and expenditures of the Federal Government."[38] On December 1, 2010, the President's Fiscal

---

[37] During Senate floor consideration of S.Con.Res. 21 in March 2007, Senator DeMint offered an amendment (S.Amdt. 489) that would have allowed for the creation of a reserve fund for Social Security reform, provided that the Senate Finance Committee approve legislation that meets certain requirements. Among other requirements, the amendment specified that such legislation must ensure "that there is no change to current law scheduled benefits for individuals born before January 1, 1951" and must provide "participants with the benefits of savings and investment while permitting the pre-funding of at least some portion of future benefits." The amendment was defeated by a vote of 45 to 52. Senator DeMint offered a similar amendment to the FY2009 budget resolution (S.Con.Res. 70) on March 13, 2008. The amendment (S.Amdt. 4328) was defeated by a vote of 41 to 57.

[38] Executive Order–National Commission on Fiscal Responsibility and Reform, February 18, 2010, available at http://www.whitehouse.gov/the-press-office/executive-order-national-commission-fiscal-responsibility-and-reform.

Commission released its final report. The recommendations proposed by the commission include Social Security program changes designed to improve benefit adequacy for certain groups while addressing long-term trust fund solvency through benefit reductions for most beneficiaries (compared with benefits scheduled under current law) and revenue increases.[39]

The proposed recommendations include changes that would increase benefits for certain beneficiaries, such as a new special minimum benefit[40] for long-term low-wage earners that would be indexed to wage growth (the benefit would be equal to 125% of the poverty level for a worker with 25 years of covered employment) and a benefit increase for older beneficiaries (i.e., a 1% increase in benefits each year from ages 82 to 86).

The proposed recommendations also include a number of benefit and revenue changes to address long-term trust fund solvency. For example, the proposal includes gradual changes to the benefit formula used to compute initial monthly benefits (making the benefit formula more progressive over time) and a gradual increase in the retirement age. Under current law, the full retirement age (FRA) is scheduled to reach age 67 for workers born in 1960 or later (i.e., it is scheduled to reach age 67 in 2027). Under the proposal, after the FRA reaches age 67, it would be further increased by one month every two years, reaching age 68 by about 2050 and age 69 by about 2075. The early eligibility age (EEA), age 62 under current law, would increase to age 63 and age 64 in step with the FRA. In conjunction with the proposed increase in the retirement age, the commission proposes a hardship exemption for those who are unable to work beyond the current EEA and may not qualify for disability benefits. The hardship exemption, which would be available for up to 20% of retirees, would allow individuals to continue to claim benefits at age 62 as the EEA and the FRA increase, with no additional actuarial reduction resulting from the increased FRA. The proposed increase in the retirement age is linked to projected increases in life expectancy. In addition, the commission recommends using a different measure of price change (the chained Consumer Price Index) to compute the Social Security COLA, on the basis that the current measure of price change used for this purpose overstates inflation.

The proposed recommendations would expand Social Security coverage by making coverage mandatory for newly hired state and local government workers after 2020. They would gradually increase the taxable wage base (the amount of covered earnings subject to the payroll tax each year) such that 90% of aggregate wages in covered employment would be taxable by 2050. The commission estimates that the taxable wage base would be about $190,000 in 2020, compared to approximately $168,000 under current law at that time.

The proposal includes other general recommendations. To provide greater flexibility in claiming benefits, the commission proposes allowing individuals to claim up to half of their benefits as early as age 62 (with the applicable actuarial reduction) and the other half at a later age. The commission directs the Social Security Administration to better inform future beneficiaries about retirement options and encourages efforts to promote greater personal savings for retirement.

Projections show that the proposed recommendations would result in lower benefits for most beneficiaries in the future compared with benefits scheduled under current law (the proposed

---

[39] *The Moment of Truth: Report of the National Commission on Fiscal Responsibility and Reform*, December 1, 2010, http://www.fiscalcommission.gov/sites/fiscalcommission.gov/files/documents/TheMomentofTruth12_1_2010.pdf (hereinafter cited as Report of the President's Fiscal Commission).

[40] For more information, see CRS Report R41518, *Social Security: The Minimum Benefit Provision*, by Alison M. Shelton.

changes would result in higher benefits for some low-wage earners).[41] In addition, projections show that the proposed recommendations would restore long-range trust fund solvency (i.e., the proposed changes would close 112% of the system's projected average 75-year funding gap).[42]

On December 3, 2010, a majority of commission members expressed support for the recommendations in the final report (11 out of 18 members), three short of the super-majority needed to require congressional action on the recommendations.

Initiatives for Change

The 1994-1996 Social Security Advisory Council presented three different approaches to restore long-range solvency to the system, none of which was endorsed by a majority of council members. The first (the "maintain benefits" plan) would maintain the system's current benefit structure by increasing revenues (including an eventual increase in the payroll tax) and making minor benefit reductions. It was also suggested that a portion of the Social Security trust funds be invested in stocks. The second (the "individual account" plan) addressed the problem mostly with benefit reductions, and would require workers to make an extra 1.6% of pay contribution to individual accounts. The third (the "personal security account" plan) proposed a major redesign of the system that would gradually replace the current earnings-related retirement benefit with a flat-rate benefit based on length of service and establish individual accounts funded by redirecting 5 percentage points of the current payroll tax. It would cover transition costs with an increase in payroll taxes of 1.52% of pay and government borrowing. The conceptual approaches incorporated in the three plans are reflected in many of the reform bills introduced in recent years.

During his last three years in office, former President Clinton repeatedly called for using Social Security's share of budget surpluses projected at the time to reduce publicly held federal debt and crediting the trust funds for the reduction.[43] In the 1999 State of the Union address, he proposed crediting $2.8 trillion of some $4.9 trillion in budget surpluses projected for the next 15 years to the trust funds—nearly $0.6 trillion was to be invested in stocks, the rest in federal securities. The plan was estimated to keep the system solvent until 2059. Concerns were raised that the plan would be crediting the Social Security trust funds twice for its surpluses, and that the plan would lead to government ownership of private companies. Former President Clinton further proposed that $0.5 trillion of the budget surpluses be used to create new Universal Savings Accounts—401(k)-type accounts intended to supplement Social Security benefits. In June 1999, he revised the plan by calling for general fund infusions to the trust funds equal to the interest savings achieved by using Social Security's share of the budget surpluses to reduce federal debt. The infusions were to be invested in stocks until the stock portion of the trust funds' holdings reached 15%. In October 1999, former President Clinton revised the plan again by dropping the stock investment idea and calling for all the infusions to be invested in federal bonds. Former President Clinton's last plan, offered in January 2000, was similar but again called for investing up to 15% of the trust funds in stocks.

---

[41] Report of the President's Fiscal Commission, p. 55.

[42] Report of the President's Fiscal Commission, p. 54.

[43] For more information, see U.S. Congress, House Committee on Ways and Means, *The President's Social Security Framework*, hearing, 106th Cong., 1st sess., February 23, 1999, Serial 106-32 (Washington: GPO, 2000).

During his first term, former President Bush appointed a commission to make recommendations to reform Social Security. As principles for reform, he stated that any reform plan must preserve the benefits of current retirees and older workers, return Social Security to a firm financial footing, and allow younger workers to invest in individual savings accounts. The commission's final report, which was issued on December 21, 2001, included three reform options. Each option would allow workers to participate in individual accounts on a voluntary basis and reduce their future Social Security benefit by the projected value of the account based on an assumed (rather than the actual) rate of return.

The first option would allow workers to redirect 2% of taxable earnings to individual accounts and would make no other changes. The second option would allow workers to redirect 4% of taxable earnings, up to an annual limit of $1,000, to individual accounts; reduce initial benefits for future retirees by indexing the growth of initial benefits to prices rather than wages; and increase benefits for lower-wage workers and widow(er)s. The third option would allow workers to contribute an additional 1% of taxable earnings to individual accounts and receive a government match of 2.5% of taxable earnings, up to an annual limit of $1,000; reduce initial benefits for future retirees by slowing the growth of initial benefits to reflect projected increases in life expectancy, and, for higher-wage workers, by modifying the benefit formula; and increase benefits for lower-wage workers and widow(er)s.[44]

During his second term, former President Bush continued efforts to build support for Social Security reform. Although the former President did not present a detailed plan for reform, he put forth guidelines for Congress to consider in the development of legislation to create individual accounts within a program that he described as in need of "wise and effective reform." During the 2005 State of the Union address, former President Bush offered the following guidelines for reform: (1) workers born before 1950 (aged 55 or older in 2005) would not be affected by individual accounts or other components of reform; (2) participation in individual accounts would be voluntary; (3) eligible workers would be allowed to redirect up to 4% of covered earnings to an individual account, initially up to $1,000 per year; (4) accounts would be administered by a centralized government entity; and (5) workers would be required to annuitize the portion of the account balance needed to provide at least a poverty-level stream of life-long income, with any remaining balance available as a lump sum.

In addition to restating support for individual accounts as part of the creation of an "ownership society," former President Bush acknowledged that other changes would be needed to address the system's projected long-range funding shortfall. He cited potential program changes that would be on the table for consideration, including (1) raising the full retirement age; (2) reducing benefits for wealthy beneficiaries; and (3) modifying the benefit formula. At the time, the only approach ruled out by former President Bush was an increase in the payroll tax rate.

On April 28, 2005, during a television news conference, former President Bush proposed a change in the Social Security benefit formula in which future "benefits for low-income workers [would] grow faster than benefits for people who are better off." Although details of the proposal were not released, a White House press statement indicated that the President was referring to a proposal similar to one put forth by Robert Pozen, a member of the 2001 *President's Commission*

---

[44] For more information, see CRS Report RL32006, *Social Security Reform: Effect on Benefits and the Federal Budget of Plans Proposed by the President's Commission to Strengthen Social Security*, by Dawn Nuschler and Geoffrey C. Kollmann.

to Strengthen Social Security appointed by former President Bush. Mr. Pozen's proposal, known as "progressive indexing," would restrain the growth of initial benefits for future retirees by using a combination of wage indexing and price indexing mechanisms in the benefit formula (rather than wage indexing only) to apply differing degrees of benefit reduction based on the worker's level of earnings.[45] Under progressive indexing, lower-wage workers would receive a benefit that is indexed closer to wage growth (as under current law) and higher-wage workers would receive a benefit that is indexed closer to price growth (or inflation). Based on current wage and price growth projections, a shift from wage indexing toward price indexing would result in lower initial benefits for many future retirees compared to current law.[46]

As the first session of the 109th Congress came to a close at the end of 2005, the reform debate focused on legislation introduced by Senator DeMint (S. 1302) that would have established voluntary individual accounts funded with surplus Social Security tax revenues and reduced Social Security benefits to reflect account assets (S. 1302 is described in the following section of the report). On November 15, 2005, Senator Santorum made unanimous consent requests to discharge S. 1302 and a second measure (S. 1750, 109th Congress) from the Senate Finance Committee and bring those measures to the Senate floor for consideration. S. 1750, introduced by Senator Santorum, would have provided for the issuance of Social Security "benefit guarantee certificates" to persons born before 1950 for the stated purpose of "guaranteeing their right to receive Social Security benefits ... in full with an accurate annual cost-of-living adjustment." The unanimous consent requests provided for 10 hours of debate on each measure followed by a vote on passage, with no amendments. Objections raised against the unanimous consent requests prevented further action on the measures.[47]

During the 2006 State of the Union address, former President Bush expressed concern regarding the level of federal spending for entitlement programs, citing projections that Social Security, Medicare, and Medicaid would account for almost 60% of the federal budget by 2030. The former President called for the creation of a commission that would include Members of Congress from both parties to "examine the full impact of baby boom retirements on Social Security, Medicare, and Medicaid." In addition, former President Bush included in his *Fiscal Year 2007 Budget* a proposal for voluntary individual accounts funded with a portion of current payroll taxes similar to the one he outlined in the 2005 State of the Union address. The *Fiscal Year 2007 Budget* also restated the former President's support for a change in the Social Security benefit formula known as "progressive indexing" to restrain the growth of initial benefits for future retirees as a cost-saving measure.

Immediately following the November 2006 congressional elections, in which Democrats gained a majority in both the House and the Senate, former President Bush and Administration officials publicly expressed interest in resuming discussions with congressional leaders on the issue of Social Security reform. In the *Fiscal Year 2009 Budget*, former President Bush restated support for voluntary individual accounts funded with a portion of current payroll taxes. Under his proposal, starting in 2013, individual accounts would be funded with 4% of taxable earnings, up

---

[45] For more information, see *Testimony on Progressive Indexing* before the Senate Finance Committee, April 26, 2005, by Robert C. Pozen.

[46] Under the trustees' 2012 intermediate projections, wages are projected to increase at an average annual rate of 3.92% over the 75-year projection period, compared with a 2.80% growth rate for prices.

[47] For more information on S. 1750, see CRS Report RL32822, *Social Security Reform: Legal Analysis of Social Security Benefit Entitlement Issues*, by Kathleen S. Swendiman and Thomas J. Nicola.

---

to a limit of $1,400 (the contribution limit would increase by $100 more than average wage growth each year through 2018). The former President also restated support for "progressive indexing" of initial Social Security benefits for future retirees.

In the 2010 State of the Union address, President Obama expressed concern regarding the federal budget outlook, including the projected growth in spending for Medicare, Medicaid, and Social Security, and called for the formation of a bipartisan fiscal commission. As discussed above, the National Commission on Fiscal Responsibility and Reform established by President Obama in February 2010 released its final report on December 1, 2010, which includes a number of proposed changes to the Social Security program. On December 3, 2010, a majority of commission members expressed support for the recommendations (11 out of 18 members), three short of the super-majority needed to require congressional action on the recommendations.

In the *Fiscal Year 2012 President's Budget*, released February 14, 2011, President Obama expressed support for bipartisan efforts "to strengthen Social Security for the future" and outlined six principles for reform. The President's budget states:

- "Any reform should strengthen Social Security for future generations and restore long-term solvency.

- The Administration will oppose any measures that privatize or weaken the Social Security system.

- While all measures to strengthen solvency should be on the table, the Administration will not accept an approach that slashes benefits for future generations.

- No current beneficiaries should see their basic benefits reduced.

- Reform should strengthen retirement security for the most vulnerable, including low-income seniors.

- Reform should maintain robust disability and survivors' benefits."[48]

On April 13, 2011, President Obama put forth a deficit reduction framework that includes references to Social Security reform. The President's document states

> The President does not believe that Social Security is a driver of our near-term deficit problems or is currently in crisis. But he supports bipartisan efforts to strengthen Social Security for the long haul, because its long-term challenges are better addressed sooner than later to ensure that it remains the rock-solid benefit for older Americans that it has been for past generations. The President in the State of the Union laid out his principles for Social Security reform which he believes should form the basis for bipartisan negotiations that could proceed in parallel to deficit negotiations:
>
> - Strengthen retirement security for the low-income and vulnerable; maintain robust disability and survivors' benefits.

---

[48] *Budget of the United States Government, Fiscal Year 2012*, released February 14, 2011, available at http://www.gpo.gov/fdsys/pkg/BUDGET-2012-BUD/pdf/BUDGET-2012-BUD.pdf, pp. 26-27. For additional information on Social Security-related proposals, see section titled "Social Security Administration," pp. 163-165.

- No privatization or weakening of the Social Security system; reform must strengthen Social Security and restore long-term solvency.

- No current beneficiary should see the basic benefit reduced; nor will we accept an approach that slashes benefits for future generations.[49]

In the *Fiscal Year 2013 President's Budget*, released February 13, 2012, President Obama stated that he is "strongly opposed to privatizing Social Security and looks forward to working on a bipartisan basis to preserve it for future generations."[50]

Legislation Introduced in the 109th Congress

During the past several Congresses, a number of Social Security reform bills have been introduced, many of which would have established individual accounts within the Social Security system either on a voluntary or mandatory basis. In the 109th Congress, 10 Social Security reform measures were introduced: H.R. 440 (Kolbe and Boyd), H.R. 530 (Johnson), H.R. 750 (Shaw), H.R. 1776 (Ryan), H.R. 2472 (Wexler), H.R. 3304 (McCrery), S. 540 (Hagel), S. 857 (Sununu), S. 1302 (DeMint), and S. 2427 (Bennett). All but two of the measures (H.R. 2472 and S. 2427) would have established individual accounts to supplement or replace traditional Social Security benefits, among other changes. This section provides a summary of Social Security reform legislation introduced in the 109th Congress, with the exception of H.R. 530, H.R. 750, S. 540 and H.R. 2472. These measures, which were re-introduced in the 110th Congress, are included in the section that follows ("Legislation Introduced in the 110th Congress"). Despite intense debate on the issue of Social Security reform in the 109th Congress, there was no congressional action on Social Security reform legislation.[51]

H.R. 440. Representatives Jim Kolbe and Allen Boyd introduced H.R. 440 (Bipartisan Retirement Security Act of 2005) on February 1, 2005. For workers under the age of 55, the measure would have redirected 3% of the first $10,000 of covered earnings (indexed to wage growth) and 2% of remaining covered earnings to mandatory individual accounts. Workers would have been allowed to make additional contributions of up to $5,000 annually (indexed to inflation), and lower-wage workers would have been eligible for an additional credit of up to $600 toward their account.

With respect to traditional Social Security benefits, the measure would have made a number of benefit computation changes, including several adjustments to the "replacement factors" used in the benefit formula. It would have constrained the growth of initial monthly benefits for future retirees by indexing initial benefits to increases in life expectancy, a provision known as "longevity indexing" of benefits. The measure would have modified the calculation of the worker's "average indexed monthly earnings" (AIME) for benefit computation purposes. In the

---

[49] *The President's Framework for Shared Prosperity and Shared Fiscal Responsibility*, April 13, 2011, at http://www.whitehouse.gov/the-press-office/2011/04/13/fact-sheet-presidents-framework-shared-prosperity-and-shared-fiscal-resp.

[50] *Budget of the United States Government, Fiscal Year 2013*, released February 13, 2012, available at http://www.whitehouse.gov/sites/default/files/omb/budget/fy2013/assets/budget.pdf, p. 195.

[51] More detailed descriptions and estimates of the financial effects of these proposals are available from the Social Security Administration, Office of the Chief Actuary, at http://www.ssa.gov/OACT/solvency/index.html.

future, the worker's AIME would have been based on the worker's average career earnings—counting all years of earnings divided by a 40-year computation period (rather than the worker's average career earnings, counting the 35 years of highest earnings divided by a 35-year computation period).

In addition, the measure would have accelerated the increase in the full retirement age from 65 to 67 scheduled under current law, so that it would have reached age 67 for persons born in 1956 or later (four years earlier than under current law). It would have modified the early retirement reduction factors and delayed retirement credits; set widow(er)s' benefits equal to 75% of the couple's combined pre-death benefit (rather than 50%-67%); limited benefits for aged spouses of higher earners; provided a minimum benefit tied to the poverty level for workers who meet specified coverage requirements; and reduced cost-of-living adjustments.

With respect to tax changes, the measure would have increased the taxable wage base gradually so that 87% of covered earnings would be taxable. It would have credited all revenues from the taxation of Social Security benefits to the Social Security trust funds (instead of crediting part to the Medicare Hospital Insurance trust fund).

H.R. 440 would have established a central authority to administer the accounts and provided initial investment options similar to those available under the Thrift Savings Plan for federal employees. Once the account balance reached $7,500 (indexed to inflation), the worker would have been allowed to choose among a broader range of centrally managed investment options. The account would have become available at retirement, or earlier if the account balance were sufficient to provide a payment at least equal to 185% of the poverty level. The worker would have been required to annuitize the portion of the account balance needed to provide a combined monthly payment (traditional benefit plus annuity) at least equal to 185% of the poverty level. Any remaining balance could have been taken as a lump sum.

H.R. 3304. Representative Jim McCrery introduced H.R. 3304 (Growing Real Ownership for Workers Act of 2005) on July 14, 2005. The measure, which is similar to S. 1302, would have established voluntary individual accounts for workers born after 1949 (workers would have been enrolled automatically in the individual account system and given the option to disenroll). Individual accounts would have been funded with general revenues in amounts equal to surplus Social Security tax revenues projected at the time from 2006 to 2016.

H.R. 3304 would have established a central authority to administer the accounts. Initially, funds would have been invested in long-term Treasury bonds. Beginning in 2009, additional investment options may have been made available. The account would have become available at retirement, or in the event of the worker's death. At retirement, the worker would have been required to annuitize the portion of the account balance needed to provide a combined monthly payment (traditional benefit plus annuity) at least equal to the poverty level. Any remaining balance could have been taken as a lump sum. For account participants, traditional Social Security benefits would have been offset by an amount equal to the annuity value of a hypothetical (or "shadow") account assumed to have earned, on average, a 2.7% real rate of return. (The assumed rate of return for the hypothetical account was based on the projected ultimate real rate of return for the Social Security trust funds (3% on average) minus 0.3 percentage point to reflect administrative expenses.) The measure would have made no other changes to traditional Social Security benefits.

S. 857/H.R. 1776. Senator John Sununu introduced S. 857 (Social Security Personal Savings Guarantee and Prosperity Act of 2005) on April 20, 2005. Representative Paul Ryan introduced a companion measure (H.R. 1776) on April 21, 2005. The measures would have allowed workers under the age of 55 to redirect a portion of payroll taxes to voluntary individual accounts (workers would have been enrolled automatically in the individual account system and given the option to disenroll). From 2006 to 2015, workers would have been allowed to redirect 5% of covered earnings up to a base amount ($10,000 in 2006, indexed to wage growth thereafter) and 2.5% of remaining covered earnings to individual accounts. Beginning in 2016, workers would have been allowed to redirect 10% of covered earnings up to the base amount and 5% of remaining covered earnings to the accounts. Workers participating in individual accounts would have been issued a "benefit credit certificate" (or recognition bond) to reflect the value of benefits accrued under the traditional system. The recognition bond would have been redeemable at retirement, though the value of accrued benefits would have been reduced to reflect the payroll taxes redirected to the worker's account. The measures would have provided account participants a combined monthly payment (traditional benefit plus annuity) at least equal to benefits scheduled under current law. Workers choosing not to participate in individual accounts would have received traditional Social Security benefits.

The measures would have provided 6 indexed investment accounts, including a default "lifecycle investment account" with an expected average investment mix of 65% equities/35% fixed income instruments. Once the worker's account balance reached $25,000 (indexed to inflation), additional investment options would have become available. At retirement, the worker would have been required to annuitize the portion of the account balance needed to provide a combined monthly payment (traditional benefit plus inflation-indexed annuity) at least equal to benefits scheduled under current law. Any excess balance could have been withdrawn in a manner chosen by the worker. Pre-retirement distribution would have been allowed if the account balance were sufficient to provide an annuity at least equal to a required minimum payment. The measures also included several financing provisions that would have constrained future growth rates for federal spending and dedicated the savings to Social Security; "reserved" annual Social Security cash flow surpluses for Social Security purposes; and dedicated a portion of projected corporate tax revenue increases to Social Security.

S. 1302. Senator Jim DeMint introduced S. 1302 (Stop the Raid on Social Security Act of 2005) on June 23, 2005. The measure would have established voluntary individual accounts for workers born after 1949 (workers would have been enrolled automatically in the individual account system and given the option to disenroll). Individual accounts would have been funded with surplus Social Security tax revenues projected at the time from 2006 to 2016. Given the redirection of surplus Social Security tax revenues to individual accounts, the measure would have provided for general revenue transfers to the trust funds in amounts needed to maintain trust fund solvency based on current-law projections.

S. 1302 would have established a central authority to administer the accounts. Initially, funds would have been invested in long-term Treasury bonds. Beginning in 2008, additional investment options may have been made available. The account would have become available at retirement, or in the event of the worker's death. At retirement, the worker would have been required to annuitize the portion of the account balance needed to provide a combined monthly payment (traditional benefit plus annuity) at least equal to the poverty level. Any remaining balance could have been taken as a lump sum. For account participants, traditional Social Security benefits would have been offset by an amount equal to the annuity value of a hypothetical (or "shadow") account assumed to have earned, on average, a 2.7% real rate of return. (The assumed rate of return for the hypothetical account was based on the projected ultimate real rate of return for the Social Security trust funds (3% on average) minus 0.3 percentage point to reflect administrative expenses.) The measure would have made no other changes to traditional Social Security benefits.

S. 2427. Senator Robert Bennett introduced S. 2427 (Sustainable Solvency First for Social Security Act of 2006) on March 16, 2006. The measure would have modified the benefit formula to provide "progressive indexing" of initial Social Security benefits for future retirees. Progressive indexing applies a combination of wage indexing and price indexing to the benefit formula that, under current projections, would result in lower benefits for workers with earnings above a certain level (with larger reductions for relatively higher earners) compared to current law. The measure would have further constrained the growth of initial Social Security benefits for future retirees by indexing initial benefits to increases in life expectancy, a provision known as "longevity indexing" of benefits. It would have accelerated the increase in the full retirement age (from 65 to 67) being phased-in under current law so that the full retirement age would have reached 67 for persons born in 1955 or later (five years earlier than under current law). The measure would have provided general revenue transfers to the Social Security trust funds as needed to maintain adequate trust fund balances.

Legislation Introduced in the 110th Congress

During the 110th Congress, six Social Security reform bills were introduced: H.R. 1090 (Lewis), H.R. 2002 (Johnson), H.R. 4181 (Flake), S. 2765 (Hagel), H.R. 5779 (Wexler) and H.R. 6110 (Ryan). H.R. 1090 (which is similar to H.R. 750 in the 109th Congress[52]) would have established voluntary individual accounts funded with general revenues, among other changes. H.R. 2002 (which is similar to H.R. 530 in the 109th Congress), H.R. 4181, S. 2765 (which is similar to S. 540 in the 109th Congress) and H.R. 6110 would have established individual accounts funded with a redirection of current payroll taxes, among other changes. H.R. 5779 (which is similar to H.R. 2472 in the 109th Congress) would have increased Social Security revenues by requiring workers and employers each to contribute 3% of earnings above the Social Security taxable wage base (in addition to payroll tax contributions under current law). This section provides a summary of Social Security reform legislation introduced in the 110th Congress, with the exception of H.R. 4181, H.R. 5779 and H.R. 6110. These measures were re-introduced in the 111th Congress and are included in the next section (see H.R. 107, H.R. 1863 and H.R. 4529 in "Legislation Introduced in the 111th Congress"). There was no congressional action on these measures during the 110th Congress.

H.R. 1090. Representative Ron Lewis introduced H.R. 1090 (Social Security Guarantee Plus Act of 2007) on February 15, 2007. The measure would have allowed workers aged 18 and older (who have been assigned a Social Security Number) to participate in voluntary individual accounts funded with general revenues. Account contributions would have been equal to 4% of taxable earnings, up to a limit of $1,000 (the limit would have been indexed to wage growth).

With respect to traditional Social Security benefits, the measure would have provided up to five years of earnings credits for workers who stay at home to care for a child under age seven and eliminated the earnings test for beneficiaries below the full retirement age. In addition, it would

---

[52] In the 109th Congress, H.R. 750 was introduced by Representative Shaw.

have set widow(er)'s benefits equal to 75% of the couple's combined pre-death benefit (compared to 50%-67% under current law); allowed widow(er)s to qualify for benefits based on a disability regardless of age and the time frame in which the disability occurred; and lowered the Social Security spousal/widow(er)'s benefit reduction under the Government Pension Offset from two-thirds to one-third of the individual's pension from noncovered employment.

Under H.R. 1090, accounts would have been administered by private financial institutions selected by the government. The measure would have provided three initial investment options with specified allocations in equities and corporate bonds (60/40, 65/35, 70/30). The account would have become available upon the worker's entitlement to retirement or disability benefits, or upon the worker's death. Upon benefit entitlement, the worker would have received a lump sum equal to 5% of the account balance. The remaining balance would have been used to finance all or part of the worker's benefit. The account balance would have been withdrawn gradually and transferred to the trust funds for the payment of monthly benefits. In addition to the 5% lump sum, the measure would have provided a monthly payment equal to the higher of a benefit scheduled under current law and an annuity based on 95% of the account balance.

H.R. 2002. Representative Sam Johnson introduced H.R. 2002 (Individual Social Security Investment Program Act of 2007) on April 23, 2007. The measure would have established individual accounts funded with 6.2 percentage points of the current Social Security payroll tax. Participation in the individual account system would have been voluntary for workers aged 22 to 54 (in 2007) and mandatory for younger individuals. Workers participating in the individual account system would no longer have accrued benefits under the current system and would have been issued a marketable "recognition bond" equal to the value of benefits already accrued. The measure would have provided workers participating in the individual account system a minimum benefit equal to a specified percentage of the poverty level, up to 100% for workers who have at least 35 years of earnings.

Workers choosing not to participate in the individual account system would have remained in the current system, however, initial monthly benefits would have been lower than those scheduled under current law. The measure would have constrained the growth of initial monthly benefits for future retirees by indexing initial benefits to price growth (rather than wage growth), a provision known as "price indexing" of benefits.

H.R. 2002 would have established a central authority to administer the accounts and provided at least three initial investment options with specified allocations in equities and fixed income instruments (government bonds and corporate bonds), including a default 60/40 investment mix. Once the account balance reached $10,000 (indexed to inflation), the worker would have been allowed to transfer the balance to a private financial institution. The account would have become available at retirement (i.e., at the Social Security full retirement age), or earlier if the account balance were sufficient to provide an annuity at least equal to 100% of the poverty level. In the case of pre-retirement account distribution, the worker would have received an annual rebate of future payroll tax contributions (the employer share of the payroll tax would not have been subject to rebate). The worker would have been required to annuitize the portion of the account balance needed to provide an annuity at least equal to 100% of the poverty level. Any remaining balance could have been taken as a lump sum. At retirement, if the account balance were not sufficient to provide the prescribed minimum payment, a supplemental payment would have been made to the account from general revenues.

S. 2765. Senator Chuck Hagel introduced S. 2765 (Saving Social Security Act of 2008) on March 13, 2008. The measure would have allowed workers born in 1963 or later (workers aged 45 or younger in 2008) to redirect 4 percentage points of the current Social Security payroll tax to an individual account (a SAFE account). Eligible workers would have been enrolled automatically in the individual account system and allowed to waive their eligibility for a SAFE account.

With respect to traditional Social Security benefits, the measure would have constrained the growth of initial benefits for future retirees by indexing initial benefits to increases in life expectancy, a provision known as "longevity indexing" of benefits. In addition, the measure would have increased the full retirement age from 67 to 68 for persons born in 1963 or later and increased the early retirement reduction factors. For workers participating in the individual account system, traditional Social Security benefits would have been offset by an amount equal to the annuity value of a hypothetical (or "shadow") account assumed to earn a 3% real rate of return. The measure would have provided a minimum "primary insurance amount" (basic benefit amount before any adjustments for early or delayed retirement) up to 135% of the poverty level for workers with 35 years of Social Security-covered employment (lower percentages would have applied to workers with fewer years of coverage).

The bill would have established a central authority to administer the individual accounts and provided initial investment options such as those offered by the Thrift Savings Plan for federal employees. The individual account would have become available at retirement, or in the event of the worker's death. Upon entitlement to benefits, the worker would have been required to annuitize the portion of the account balance needed to provide a combined monthly payment (traditional benefit plus annuity) at least equal to 135% of the poverty level. Any remaining balance could have been withdrawn in a manner chosen by the worker.

Legislation Introduced in the 111th Congress

During the 111th Congress, four Social Security reform bills were introduced: H.R. 107 (Flake), S. 426 (Bennett), H.R. 1863 (Wexler) and H.R. 4529 (Ryan). This section provides a summary of these measures. There was no congressional action on these measures during the 111th Congress.

H.R. 107. Representative Jeff Flake introduced H.R. 107 (Securing Medicare and Retirement for Tomorrow Act of 2009) on January 6, 2009.[53] Among other provisions, the measure would have established individual accounts funded with 6.2 percentage points of the current Social Security payroll tax. Participation in the individual account system would have been mandatory for workers below the Social Security full retirement age. At retirement, workers would have been allowed to choose between a Social Security retirement benefit (Part A retirement benefit payable to workers and spouses) and a retirement distribution from the individual account (Part B benefit). Part A retirement benefits would have been phased-out over time. Individuals reaching retirement age after a period of 42 calendar years following enactment of the bill would not have had the option of choosing Part A retirement benefits.[54]

---

[53] H.R. 107 is similar to H.R. 4181 introduced by Representative Flake in the 110th Congress.

[54] The measure also would have made changes to the Medicare program in connection with the establishment of Social Security individual accounts.

The worker's individual account would have been maintained by the employer and contributions would have been invested in a qualified Social Security mutual fund. Workers would have designated an investment fund from among five qualified Social Security mutual funds selected by the employer.

H.R. 107 would have established a Social Security Escrow Fund within the U.S. Treasury. The fund would have included securities held by the Social Security trust funds, 6.2 percentage points of the current Social Security payroll tax, Medicare Hospital Insurance (HI) payroll taxes, and amounts appropriated for the Supplemental Security Income (SSI) program, among other funding sources.[55] Amounts held in the Social Security Escrow Fund would have been available for the payment of various types of Social Security benefits—including Part A retirement benefits, benefits payable to a worker's family members (such as children and surviving spouses), disability benefits, and lump-sum death benefits—as well as for the payment of SSI benefits. In addition, transfers would have been made from the fund to the Medicare HI trust fund in the amount of Medicare Part A benefits.

The measure would have established the Personal Accounts Management and Review Board as an independent agency within the executive branch of the government. Among other duties, the board would have operated the Social Security Escrow Fund and designated and regulated qualified Social Security mutual funds. The Secretary of the Treasury would have served as managing trustee of the Social Security Escrow Fund.

S. 426. Senator Robert Bennett introduced S. 426 (Social Security Solvency Act of 2009) on February 12, 2009.[56] The measure would have modified the benefit formula to provide "progressive indexing" of initial Social Security benefits for future retirees. Progressive indexing applies a combination of wage indexing and price indexing to the benefit formula that, under current projections, would result in lower benefits for workers with earnings above a certain level (with larger reductions for relatively higher earners) compared to current law. The measure would have further constrained the growth of initial benefits for future retirees by indexing initial benefits to increases in life expectancy, a provision known as "longevity indexing" of benefits. In addition, it would have accelerated the increase in the full retirement age (from 65 to 67) being phased-in under current law so that the full retirement age would have reached 67 for persons born in 1955 or later (five years earlier than under current law). The measure would have provided general revenue transfers to the Social Security trust funds as needed to maintain adequate trust fund balances.

H.R. 1863. Representative Robert Wexler introduced H.R. 1863 (Social Security Forever Act of 2009) on April 1, 2009.[57] The measure would have increased Social Security revenues by requiring workers and employers each to contribute 3% of covered earnings above the Social Security taxable wage base, in addition to the payroll tax contributions payable under current law.

Under current law, workers and employers each contribute 6.2% of covered earnings up to the taxable wage base. The taxable wage base, which increases each year according to average wage

---

[55] If an individual had elected to receive Part A retirement benefits (in lieu of Part B benefits), the qualified Social Security mutual fund in which the individual's account contributions were invested would have been required to transfer the amount of the individual's Part B benefits to the Social Security Escrow Fund.

[56] S. 426 is similar to S. 2427 introduced by Senator Bennett in the 109th Congress.

[57] Former Representative Robert Wexler retired from Congress in January 2010.

---

growth if a Social Security COLA is payable, is $110,100 in 2012. Earnings up to the taxable wage base (earnings on which payroll tax contributions are paid) are credited for benefit computation purposes.

Under the measure, workers and employers each would have been required to contribute 3% of earnings *above* the taxable wage base, in addition to the 6.2% of earnings *up to* the taxable wage base payable under current law. Earnings above the taxable wage base taxed at the 3% rate would not have been credited for benefit computation purposes.

H.R. 4529. Representative Paul Ryan introduced H.R. 4529 (Roadmap for America's Future Act of 2010) on January 27, 2010, to provide for the reform of health care, the Social Security system, the tax code for individuals and business, job training, and the budget process.[58] Title IV of the bill (Social Security Personal Savings Guarantee and Prosperity Act of 2010) would have allowed workers aged 55 or younger in 2012 to redirect a portion of their payroll tax contributions to voluntary individual accounts. From 2012 to 2021, workers would have been allowed to redirect 2% of taxable earnings up to a base amount ($10,000 in 2012, indexed to average wage growth thereafter) and 1% of remaining taxable earnings to an individual account. The amount of Social Security contributions to be redirected to an individual account would have increased over time. From 2022 to 2031, workers would have been allowed to redirect 4% of taxable earnings up to the base amount and 2% of remaining taxable earnings. From 2032 to 2041, workers would have been allowed to redirect 6% of taxable earnings up to the base amount and 3% of remaining taxable earnings. For calendar years after 2041, workers would have been allowed to redirect 8% of taxable earnings up to the base amount and 4% of remaining taxable earnings to an individual account.

Workers choosing to participate in the individual account system would have been issued a "benefit credit certificate" to reflect the value of benefits accrued under the traditional system. The benefit credit certificate would have been redeemable at retirement and the value of accrued benefits would have been reduced to reflect the payroll taxes redirected to the worker's individual account. The measure would have provided a guarantee by the government that the value of a participant's individual account would be at least equal to the sum of his or her contributions to the account, adjusted for inflation. Workers choosing not to participate in the individual account system would have received traditional benefits (subject to changes to the system).

The measure would have provided six indexed investment accounts, including a default "lifecycle investment account." Once the worker's account balance reached a specified threshold ($25,000 in 2012, indexed to inflation thereafter), additional investment options would have become available. The account would have become available at retirement, or earlier if the account balance were sufficient to provide an annuity at least equal to 150% of the poverty line. At retirement, the worker would have been required to annuitize the portion of the account balance needed to provide a monthly payment at least equal to 150% of the poverty line, and any excess balance could have been withdrawn in a manner chosen by the worker. Any funds remaining in the account at the time of the individual's death would have been payable to designated beneficiaries or to the individual's estate.

---

[58] H.R. 4529 is similar to H.R. 6110 introduced by Representative Ryan in the 110th Congress and includes provisions similar to H.R. 1776 introduced by Representative Ryan in the 109th Congress.

Among other changes, the measure would have modified the Social Security benefit formula to provide "progressive price indexing" of initial monthly benefits for future retirees (the change would have applied to workers aged 55 or younger in 2011). Progressive price indexing applies a combination of wage indexing and price indexing to the benefit formula that is projected to result in lower initial monthly benefits for workers with earnings above a certain level (with larger benefit reductions for relatively higher earners) compared to current law. In addition, the measure would have accelerated the increase in the full retirement age (FRA) scheduled under current law, so that the FRA would have reached 67 for persons born in 1959 (one year earlier than under current law). It would have further increased the FRA for persons born in later years to reflect projected increases in life expectancy.[59]

Legislation Introduced in the 112th Congress

During the 112th Congress, several Social Security reform measures have been introduced, including H.R. 539 (Deutch), H.R. 797 (DeFazio), S. 804 (Graham, Paul, and Lee), S. 1213 (Hutchison), H.R. 2889 (McCotter), S. 1558 (Sanders), and S. 3533 (Hutchison). This section provides a summary of these measures.[60]

H.R. 539. Representative Theodore Deutch introduced H.R. 539, Preserving Our Promise to Seniors Act, on February 8, 2011. Among other provisions, the measure would gradually eliminate the taxable wage base, making all covered earnings subject to the Social Security payroll tax (12.4%) in 2018 and later. The additional taxable earnings would be counted for benefit computation purposes using a modified benefit formula. The measure would base the Social Security COLA on the Consumer Price Index for the Elderly (CPI-E) and provide a supplemental payment to Social Security and other beneficiaries in years for which no COLA is payable. It would create a point of order against legislation that would "privatize" Social Security or reduce Social Security benefits.

H.R. 797. Representative Peter DeFazio introduced H.R. 797, the No Loopholes in Social Security Taxes Act, on February 18, 2011. In addition to the current 12.4% Social Security payroll tax on earnings in covered employment up to the taxable wage base under current law, the measure would apply the 12.4% Social Security payroll tax to earnings in covered employment in excess of $250,000 beginning in calendar year 2012. The additional taxable earnings (earnings above the taxable wage base under current law) would not be counted for benefit computation purposes.[61]

S. 804. Senators Lindsey Graham, Rand Paul, and Mike Lee introduced S. 804, Social Security Solvency and Sustainability Act, on April 13, 2011. The measure would increase the full retirement age (FRA) by three months each year, beginning with persons who attain age 62 in 2017, until the FRA reaches age 70. After the FRA reaches age 70 (for persons who attain age 62 in 2032), the FRA would be increased further by about one month every two years to maintain a

---

[59] For more information, see Congressional Budget Office, *An Analysis of the Roadmap for America's Future Act of 2010*, January 27, 2010, available at http://www.cbo.gov/ftpdocs/108xx/doc10851/01-27-Ryan-Roadmap-Letter.pdf.

[60] Generally, the Social Security reform bills included here are those that have been scored by the Social Security Administration's Office of the Chief Actuary as restoring long-range solvency to the Social Security trust funds.

[61] Social Security Administration, Office of the Chief Actuary, Memo to the Honorable Peter DeFazio on H.R. 797, March 3, 2011, available at http://www.ssa.gov/OACT/solvency/index.html.

constant ratio of expected retirement years to potential working years. In addition, the earliest eligibility age (EEA) would be increased from age 62 to age 64. The EEA would be increased by three months each year, beginning with persons who attain age 62 in 2021. The EEA would reach age 64 for persons who attain age 62 in 2028 or later. The measure would modify the Social Security benefit formula to provide "progressive price indexing" of initial monthly benefits for future retirees. Progressive price indexing applies a combination of wage indexing and price indexing to the benefit formula that is projected to result in lower initial monthly benefits for workers with earnings above a certain level compared with current law (with larger benefit reductions for relatively higher earners).[62]

S. 1213. Senator Kay Bailey Hutchison introduced S. 1213, Defend and Save Social Security Act, on June 16, 2011. The measure would increase the full retirement age by three months each year, beginning with persons who attain age 62 in 2016, until the FRA reaches age 69 for persons who attain age 62 in 2027 or later. The earliest eligibility age would be increased from age 62 to age 64. The EEA would be increased by three months each year, beginning with persons who attain age 62 in 2016, until the EEA reaches age 64 for persons who attain age 62 in 2023 or later. Under the measure, the annual Social Security COLA would be computed as under current law and reduced by 1 percentage point (but not to less than zero).[63] (See related measure S. 3533 described below.)

H.R. 2889. Representative Thaddeus McCotter introduced H.R. 2889, a bill to reform Social Security by establishing a Personal Social Security Savings Program, on September 12, 2011. Among other provisions, the measure would establish a system of voluntary personal accounts for workers under the age of 50 in 2012 (persons born in 1962 or earlier). The accounts would be funded with general revenues in an amount equal to (1) 5% of earnings subject to the Social Security payroll tax, up to $10,000 in 2012, plus (2) 2.5% of taxable earnings above that amount. For years after 2012, the $10,000 threshold would be indexed to average wage growth.

The personal account system would be administered by a central authority similar to the Thrift Savings Plan for federal employees. Withdrawals from the accounts would be allowed when a participant attains the earliest eligibility age for retirement benefits (age 62 for retired workers) or when a disabled worker beneficiary attains the full retirement age. Traditional Social Security benefits (retirement and aged survivor benefits) would be reduced by up to 50% for those who participate in the personal account system. Under the proposal, account participants would be guaranteed a combined monthly payment (i.e., a reduced Social Security benefit plus an annuity based on the personal account) at least equal to the Social Security benefit that would be payable had the beneficiary not participated in the personal account system. The cost of the benefit guarantee would be funded with general revenues.

The proposal would provide authority for the Social Security trust funds to borrow from the general fund of the Treasury if needed to pay benefits on time should the trust funds become exhausted. In addition, the proposal would provide for excess Social Security trust fund income (i.e., income above what is needed to maintain a level of assets equal to annual program costs) to

---

[62] Social Security Administration, Office of the Chief Actuary, Memo to Senator Graham, Senator Paul and Senator Lee on S. 804, April 13, 2011, available at http://www.ssa.gov/OACT/solvency/index.html.

[63] Social Security Administration, Office of the Chief Actuary, Memo to the Honorable Kay Bailey Hutchison, June 9, 2011, available at http://www.ssa.gov/OACT/solvency/index.html.

be redirected to the general fund of the Treasury to help finance personal account contributions and the cost of the benefit guarantee.[64]

S. 1558. Senator Bernard Sanders introduced S. 1558 on September 14, 2011. The measure, which is similar to H.R. 797 described above, would apply the 12.4% Social Security payroll tax to earnings in covered employment in excess of $250,000 beginning in 2012. Earnings in covered employment up to the taxable wage base under current law would continue to be subject to the 12.4% payroll tax. The additional taxable earnings (earnings above the current-law taxable wage base) would not be counted for benefit computation purposes.[65]

S. 3533. Senator Kay Bailey Hutchison introduced S. 3533, Defend and Save Social Security Act of 2012, on September 12, 2012. The measure would increase the full retirement age by three months each year, beginning with persons who attain age 62 in 2016, until the FRA reaches age 70 for persons who attain age 62 in 2031 or later. The earliest eligibility age would be increased from age 62 to age 64. The EEA would be increased by three months each year, beginning with persons who attain age 62 in 2016, until the EEA reaches age 64 for persons who attain age 62 in 2023 or later. Under the measure, the annual Social Security COLA would be computed as under current law and reduced by 1 percentage point (but not to less than zero).[66] (See related measure S. 1213 described above.)

Author Contact Information

Dawn Nuschler
Specialist in Income Security
dnuschler@crs.loc.gov, 7-6283

---

[64] Social Security Administration, Office of the Chief Actuary, Memo to the Honorable Thaddeus McCotter, September 12, 2011, available at http://www.ssa.gov/OACT/solvency/index.html.

[65] Social Security Administration, Office of the Chief Actuary, Memo to the Honorable Bernard Sanders, September 7, 2011, available at http://www.ssa.gov/OACT/solvency/index.html.

[66] Social Security Administration, Office of the Chief Actuary, Memo to the Honorable Kay Bailey Hutchison, September 12, 2012, available at http://www.ssa.gov/OACT/solvency/index.html.